KURSK 1943

TIDE TURNS IN THE EAST

MARK HEALY

OSPREY
HISTORY

For my son, Benjamin

▲*Tiger and prey! No image better symbolizes the German effort during 'Citadel' than the Tiger 1 executing great destruction at long range with its 8.8cm gun. It is a measure of its effectiveness as a weapon that it could generate such an association, given that only 146 Tigers were actually employed during the offensive. Of the approximately 40 Tigers lost in July 1943, most were lost at Kursk. This example belonged to 3rd SS Panzer Grenadier Division 'Totenkopf', which served as part of II SS Panzer Corps in Fourth Panzer Army during the battle. (Bundesarchiv)*

Acknowledgements
I should like to thank the many people who gave of their time and assistance in many ways to help me with this book, in particular, Gordon Tweedle, David Farell and Alfred Umhay. Most particularly I must thank Marcus Jaugitz who very generously allowed me to use a number of photographs from his remarkable collection. Thanks also to David Fletcher of the Tank Museum, the staff of the Bundsarchiv and the Novosti Press Agency. Last, but not least, very special thanks to my wife, who put up with my frustrations, and to our son, Benjamin, who showed a remarkable tolerance of his father's absence from the family outings at weekends and during school holidays.

FOR A CATALOGUE OF ALL BOOKS PUBLISHED BY OSPREY MILITARY, AUTOMOTIVE AND AVIATION PLEASE WRITE TO:

The Marketing Manager, Osprey Direct USA, PO Box 130, Sterling Heights, MI 48311-0130, USA.
Email: info@ospreydirectusa.com

The Marketing Manager, Osprey Direct UK, PO Box 140, Wellingborough, Northants, NN8 4ZA, United Kingdom.
Email: info@ospreydirect.co.uk

Visit Osprey at:
www.ospreypublishing.com

CONTENTS

First published in Great Britain in 1993 by Osprey Publishing, Elms Court, Chapel Way, Botley, Oxford OX2 9LP United Kingdom
Email: info@ospreypublishing.com

Also published as Campaign 16: *Kursk 1943*

© 1993 Osprey Publishing Ltd.
00 01 02 03 04 10 9 8 7 6 5 4 3 2 1

Colour illustration credits: Jeffrey Burn, 59; Cilla Eurich, 18 and 26; David E. Smith, 23, 30, 63, 71, 75; Pilot Press, 67; Ron Volstad, 46; Steven J. Zaloga, 55, 83.

ISBN 1 84176 103 6

Produced by DAG Publications Ltd for Osprey Publishing Ltd.
Colour bird's eye view illustrations by Cilla Eurich.
Cartography by Micromap.
Wargaming Kursk by Andrew Grainger.
Wargames consultant Duncan Macfarlane.
Typeset by Ronset Typesetters, Darwen, Lancashire.
Mono camerawork by M&E Reproductions, North Fambridge, Essex.
Printed in China through World Print Ltd.

FRONT COVER: T-34 tanks and infantry attacking through German artillery fire near Prokhorovka between Kursk and Kharkov, August 1943. (© Novosti, London)

BACK COVER: SS Panzer Grenadiers take a break during the battle of Kursk. (R. Tomasi)

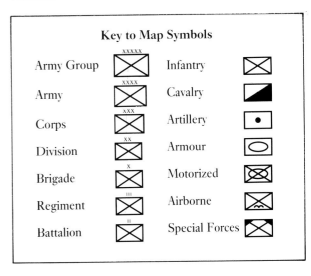

Key to Map Symbols

Army Group	XXXXX		Infantry	
Army	XXXX		Cavalry	
Corps	XXX		Artillery	•
Division	XX		Armour	
Brigade	X		Motorized	
Regiment	III		Airborne	
Battalion	II		Special Forces	

The Kursk Salient:
German Offensive Intentions and Soviet Dispositions

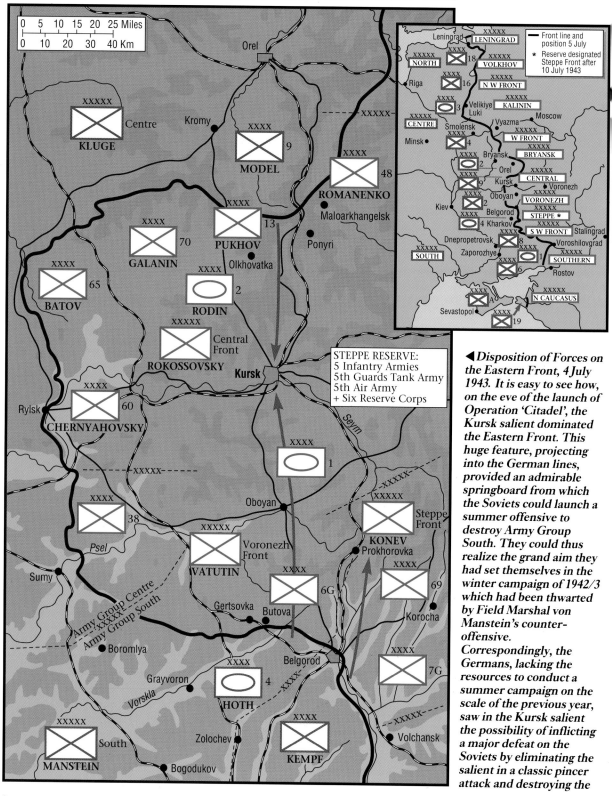

0   5   10   15   20   25 Miles
0   10   20   30   40 Km

Orel

XXXXX
Centre
KLUGE

Kromy

XXXX
9
MODEL

XXXX
48
ROMANENKO

Maloarkhangelsk

XXXX
70
GALANIN

XXXX
13
PUKHOV

Ponyri

XXXX
65
BATOV

Olkhovatka

XXXX
2
RODIN

XXXXX
Central
Front
ROKOSSOVSKY

Kursk

STEPPE RESERVE:
5 Infantry Armies
5th Guards Tank Army
5th Air Army
+ Six Reserve Corps

Rylsk

XXXX
60
CHERNYAHOVSKY

Seym

XXXX
1

XXXX
38

Psel

Oboyan

XXXXX
Voronezh
Front
VATUTIN

Steppe
Front
KONEV
Prokhorovka

Sumy

Army Group Centre
Army Group South

Gertsovka

XXXX
6G
Butova

XXXX
69
Korocha

Boromlya

Grayvoron

XXXX
4
HOTH

Belgorod

XXXX
7G

Vorskla

XXXXX
South
MANSTEIN

Zolochev

XXXX
KEMPF

Volchansk

Bogodukov

Inset map:

— Front line and
position 5 July
* Reserve designated
Steppe Front after
10 July 1943

Leningrad — XXXXX LENINGRAD
XXXXX NORTH — XXXX 18 — XXXXX VOLKHOV
Riga — XXXX 16 N W FRONT
XXXXX CENTRE — XXXX 3 Velikiye Luki — XXXXX KALININ
Moscow
Smolensk — Vyazma — XXXXX W FRONT
Minsk — XXXX 4 — XXXXX BRYANSK
Bryansk — XXXX 2
Orel — XXXX 9 Kursk — XXXXX CENTRAL
Voronezh
Oboyan — XXXXX VORONEZH
Kiev — XXXX 2
Belgorod — XXXXX STEPPE *
XXXX 4 Kharkov — XXXXX S W FRONT
Dnepropetrovsk — XXXX 8 Voroshilovgrad — Stalingrad
XXXXX SOUTH Zaporozhye — XXXX 1 — XXXXX SOUTHERN
XXXX 6 — Rostov
XXXX A — XXXXX N CAUCASUS
Sevastopol — XXXX 19

◀ *Disposition of Forces on the Eastern Front, 4 July 1943. It is easy to see how, on the eve of the launch of Operation 'Citadel', the Kursk salient dominated the Eastern Front. This huge feature, projecting into the German lines, provided an admirable springboard from which the Soviets could launch a summer offensive to destroy Army Group South. They could thus realize the grand aim they had set themselves in the winter campaign of 1942/3 which had been thwarted by Field Marshal von Manstein's counter-offensive. Correspondingly, the Germans, lacking the resources to conduct a summer campaign on the scale of the previous year, saw in the Kursk salient the possibility of inflicting a major defeat on the Soviets by eliminating the salient in a classic pincer attack and destroying the*

THE ORIGINS OF THE BATTLE

It was with the onset of the 'rasputitsa' – the great thaw that presages the return of spring to Russia – in mid-March of 1943 that the die for the great battle of Kursk was cast. The rising temperatures turned rivers, now being fed by the thawing snow, into unbridgeable torrents and the roads into quagmires, impassable to man and machine alike. For the SS Panzer Corps, the cutting edge of the German counter-offensive in the Ukraine, any advance northwards beyond Belgorod floundered to a halt in a countryside transformed into a sea of mud and in the face of rapidly hardening Soviet resistance. While the exhausted German and Soviet armies took advantage of the temporary lull imposed on them by nature, to rest and refit after the prodigious exertions of the winter, planning was already under way as to how the war in Russia was to be prosecuted come the onset of the warmer weather. As the planning staffs of STAVKA and OKH pondered the possibilities, their deliberations were governed by a number of consider-ations which were to have a major impact on their unfolding designs.

For Nazi Germany and Soviet Russia, the war in the East had reached a point of stasis. Both were driven by the realization that the result of the inevitable clash of arms between the Wehrmacht and the Red Army, in the summer of 1943, would be decisive in determining the outcome of the war on the Eastern Front. It would also contribute, in a profound manner, to the resolution of the wider conflict between the Axis and Allied powers in Europe.

After two summer campaigns Germany had not succeeded in destroying the Soviet Army. Indeed, by the spring of 1943 there was a tacit acceptance among many senior officers on the General Staff and in the Ostheer that it was increasingly unlikely that Germany could win the war in the East by defeating Soviet Russia. At issue now, was what manner of strategy the Wehrmacht could adopt for the summer of 1943, that would prevent its defeat and ensure the best outcome given the circumstances, that of a draw which would force the Soviet Union into a political accommodation with Germany. For the Soviet Union, having weathered the great and nearly fatal storms of 1941 and 1942, national survival was no longer in doubt. Unable to secure the decisive victory over the Wehrmacht in southern Russia that Stalin had so desperately desired in the winter campaign of 1942/3, the priority of Soviet strategy for the 1943 summer campaign became that of the destruction of the capacity of the Wehrmacht to withstand the growing offensive power of the Red Army. Furthermore, in neither camp was there any doubt that the southern sector was the major theatre of decision for the whole of the Eastern Front. In neither the Northern nor Central sectors were such important military, political and econo-mic matters in contention. So, as they pored over

forces therein. However, what was seen in April as a rapid and limited offensive, conducted by limited forces, by July had acquired a momentum of its own, transforming the battle that began there on 5 July 1943 into the decisive battle of the European War.

Inset: The Kursk Salient. German Offensive Intentions and Soviet Dispositions The Operational Plan for 'Citadel' was simple – the well-proven formula of the 'pincer' attack, rapidly to defeat the Soviet forces deployed in the salient. However, the forces the

Soviets had placed there, within an incredibly complex and deep defensive system, were specifically designed to 'bleed white' the mass of armour which would spearhead the German offensive drive. With their deeply echeloned forces within the salient itself, and the ability to call on the largest reserve that STAVKA had ever assembled, the Reserve (Steppe) Front, the Soviets were optimistic that they could contain 'Citadel' and thereafter go over to the offensive themselves.

the situation maps of Southern Russia, it is hardly surprising that the gaze of German and Russian alike should become fixated on the great salient to the north of Kharkov and centred on the ancient city of Kursk.

Projecting from the Soviet into the German lines like a fist, and with a frontage of some 250 miles but a mere 70 miles across its base, this massive feature, with a total land area roughly half the size of England, very quickly came to dominate the plans of STAVKA and the OKH. To the Germans and Russians alike, the great salient, so pregnant with military possibilities, became the focus of effort and intentions whose climax was to lead to one of the greatest battles of the Second World War and whose outcome was to seal the fate of Hitler's 'thousand-year Reich'.

Even as Generalfeldmarschall von Manstein's counter-stroke against the over-extended Soviet forces racing for the River Dnieper was beginning in late February of 1943, tentative discussions had already begun concerning the shape of the summer campaign. It was apparent, however, that the options being considered by Hitler, OKH and von Manstein were far less ambitious in scope than in previous years. Although by the onset of the thaw the German offensive had inflicted a major defeat on the Soviets and had given back to the Germans, if only temporarily, the initiative in the south, nothing could disguise the fact that at Stalingrad and in the subsequent drive westwards from the Volga, the Red Army had inflicted grievous losses on the Wehrmacht. It was the reality of some

▼ When Guderian described Field Marshal Erich von Manstein as 'our finest operational brain' he was expressing a sentiment shared by many in the German Army, and even Hitler had a profound respect for his abilities. But it was Hitler's refusal to countenance von Manstein's suggestion that the Soviets be allowed to begin the offensive in 1943, and then use the refitted panzer divisions, allied to the proven German expertise in mobile operations, to hit the over-extended Soviet divisions on the 'backhand', that led directly to the débâcle of Kursk. In the aftermath of the German defeat von Manstein conducted a skilful retreat throughout the remainder of 1943. Hitler finally removed him from his command of Army Group South in March 1944. (Bundesarchiv)

twenty-six divisions wiped from the German Army order of battle between January and March 1943 that gave form and shape to the strategic deliberations concerning the forthcoming summer campaign. Strength returns indicated that by March the Army was short of 470,000 men in the East alone, while the figure for all theatres revealed that the Feldheer was 700,000 men below establishment. In January 1943 a call from OKW for 800,000 men to be found for service in the Wehrmacht netted only half that figure, and it was symptomatic of the relative decline in Germany's manpower strength that many of these were drafted from the vital war industries.

In addition, the panzer divisions, the main offensive weapon of the German Army and the instrument of victory in the years of expansion, was in a deplorable state. By the end of the winter of 1943 barely 600 machines were available for service in the eighteen panzer divisions operating along the whole of the Eastern Front. Unless there were a radical overhaul of the panzer arm and a significant increase in its size and effectiveness, the Wehrmacht in Russia would be overwhelmed by the flood of Soviet armour issuing from the great tank factories beyond the Urals.

To address this vital task, Hitler recalled General Heinz Guderian in February 1943 and appointed him 'Inspector-General of Armoured Troops'; his brief being the fundamental overhaul and revamping of the panzer arm. At a Führer Conference on 9 March Guderian argued that Germany should forego any strategic offensive on the Eastern Front in 1943, in favour of building up the strength of the panzer divisions. For Guderian it was axiomatic that the rehabilitation of the panzer arm and the creation of a strong and effective armoured reserve were essential if Germany's longer-term survival, both on the Eastern Front and in the West, were to be ensured. Adoption of such a policy would enable the German Army to resume the offensive in 1944, with armoured units properly equipped for the task. To achieve this end it was militarily desirable that the German Army adopt a policy of strategic defence in the East throughout 1943.

Herein lay the quandary for the Germans. Politically, Hitler needed a great military *coup* to reassure his allies, some of whom had already begun to believe that they had backed the wrong horse. Furthermore, a defensive posture would scarcely induce Turkey to enter the war on the side of the Axis powers, a political objective of high priority for Hitler. Nor was the doctrine of strategic defence as simple in practice as it appeared desirable in theory. The great loss of manpower during the winter campaign, precluded the possibility of a passive, static defence; there were simply not enough divisions available for the task. How then, was the German Army to respond to the growing power of the Red Army, and the summer offensive it was assumed that Stalin would launch as soon as he was ready? It was von Manstein's view that Germany's only salvation in the East lay in the concept of an 'elastic' defence that exploited to the full the tactical expertise of German command staffs and the undoubted fighting qualities of the troops. Above all, it would depend on employing to the full their repeatedly demonstrated expertise in mobile operations. This would entail 'dealing the enemy powerful blows of a localized nature which would sap his strength to a decisive degree – first and foremost through losses in prisoners'. Von Manstein's proviso, however, was that the time available to Germany to deliver such blows against the Red Army was very short. Offensive action would need to be taken quickly, before Soviet military strength became overwhelming. In addition, the anticipated collapse of the Axis position in Tunisia, would be followed shortly thereafter by an Allied invasion of southern Europe. With the bulk of the Wehrmacht

◀ General Heinz Guderian had made his opposition to 'Citadel' known from the very start. Having been appointed as Inspector-General of Armoured Troops in April 1943, he succeeded, despite the Byzantine politics of Hitler's 'court', in rebuilding the panzer arm. 'Leave it alone,' he told Hitler. In the type of battle that the Soviets were imposing on the Germans, Guderian could see the very conditions that would lead to the destruction of the panzer divisions, refitted and rebuilt with such care following the defeat at Stalingrad. The outcome, he felt, must lead to the loss of the strategic initiative on the Eastern Front and with it the future of the war which would in consequence be settled in the Soviet Union's favour. (Imperial War Museum)

serving in Russia, it would be to the already hard pressed Ostheer, that Hitler would turn for divisions to counter such landings. Time was therefore of the essence. At best Germany had only a few months, following the return of the dry weather in the East, to inflict a major defeat on the Red Army, before the presence of a large Allied force on the European mainland placed a dead hand on operations on the Eastern Front.

By mid-March the decision had, in principle, been made. Rejecting other possibilities, Hitler determined that as soon as the weather was suitable he would launch Operation 'Citadel', a combined attack on the Kursk salient by Army Groups Centre and South. In a classic pincer operation, the salient would be eliminated and the enemy force therein extinguished. Much, it was assumed, would flow from this success. The destruction of Soviet units, particularly armour, would seriously disrupt the coming Soviet summer offensive and the prisoners netted would be removed to Germany as slave labour for the war economy. Such a rapid victory would also go far, Hitler believed, in demonstrating to wavering allies that Germany could still win the war and cause Turkey finally to declare for the Axis. In the wake of the successful offensive, the front line would be straightened, allowing for a more economical use of divisions in defence. Those released would form a reserve which could be deployed, if needed, to respond to the Allied landings in southern Europe. Furthermore, a rapidly executed attack would conserve the strength of the valuable panzer units and preserve them for future use. On 15 April the rationale and design for 'Citadel' was set forth in Operation Order No. 6. No one reading the document could be in any doubt that it was imperative for the operation to succeed, but success would depend on rapid execution. The fact that this rapidity was not achieved – delay after delay, as spring moved into the high summer of 1943 – has too frequently been laid at Hitler's door, the assumption being that he was the arbiter of the events that were about to unfold. But the fact is that the ruin of 'Citadel' had already been ensured by decisions taken in Moscow many months before the panzers finally rolled across their start-lines in July.

For the Russians, the clearest indications that the Germans intended to launch an early offensive, came with the thaw in March. The deployment of strong enemy forces, particularly panzer and motorized infantry units at the northern and southern necks of the Kursk salient, pointed to a German intention to eliminate it by a concentric attack. In this appreciation of German intentions, Stalin received overwhelming verification through reports from 'Lucy', the Swiss-based Soviet agent, who had access on an almost daily basis to the deliberations of the German High Command (OKW). Thus, by early April Stalin had knowledge of the substance of Hitler's Operation Order No. 6 ('Citadel'). Printed on the 15th, only thirteen copies of the document were made available, and these for the eyes of senior commanders only. The substance of 'Lucy's' Intelligence was further confirmed by an independent source when, at the end of March, the British forwarded via their Military Mission in Moscow information concerning German offensive intentions against the Kursk salient. The Russians were not told, however, that the information came from the reading and interpretation of Luftwaffe 'Enigma' transmissions by the Ultra team at Bletchley Park in England.

In early April Marshal Zhukov submitted to Stalin a major report based on information obtained from a wide-ranging reconnaissance of German dispositions and reserves initiated by the General Staff at the end of March. As a preface to his recommendations he identified the rationale for a German offensive against the Kursk salient, in terms very similar to those used by the Germans themselves, but concluded that there was little point in the Red Army pre-empting the German offensive with one of its own. Rather, Zhukov concluded, 'it will be better if we wear the enemy out in defensive action, destroy his tanks, and then, taking in fresh reserves, by going over to an all-out offensive, we will finish off the enemy's main grouping'. This then was the thrust of the case presented to Stalin at the major STAVKA conference on the evening of 12 April. According to Zhukov, 'Stalin listened as never before' and, by the end of the conference, the essential strategic decision that would determine the outcome of

'Citadel' had been taken. Shelving the STAVKA plan for the offensive that Hitler and his generals had been so right in assuming the Russians had intended to launch, Stalin acceded to the case argued by Zhukov and the Front commanders, that the German offensive should be met and ground down in a deliberately defensive battle, with the destruction of the German armour being the primary aim. As the orders flowed from STAVKA to transform the Kursk salient into one immense fortress, there were few among the Soviet generals who doubted that in the ferocious and cruel battle to come, the decisive moment of the war against Nazi Germany, had at last arrived.

▶ *Marshal of the Soviet Union Georgi Konstantinovich Zhukov, regarded as one of the 20th century's greatest soldiers. He never lost a battle. There was never any doubt in his mind that the purpose of the Soviet defensive strategy within the Kursk salient was quite simply to ensure the destruction of the German armour. Both he and Stalin knew that Germany's defeat would take time and a very great expenditure of human and matériel resources, but were certain that the destruction of the panzer divisions in the Kursk salient would prevent the Germans from ever recovering the strategic initiative on the Eastern Front. (Novosti)*

▲ Nikolai Vatutin was the commander of the Voronezh Front, which would have to absorb the offensive power of Army Group South. Following the German invasion he was chief of staff of the North-western Front. From May to July 1942 he was deputy chief of the general staff and STAVKA's representative on the Bryansk Front. In July 1942 he was appointed commander of the Voronezh Front. During the battle for Stalingrad he commanded the South-western Front and was once more appointed to the Voronezh Front in March 1943. He is seen here with Nikita Khrushchev, the future Soviet leader, who was then Military Council Member for the Voronezh Front and who played a significant role in the battle. His jovial appearance belied a ruthless capacity and will to exercise his power as Stalin's political representative when the need arose, as it did on at least two occasions during the course of the battle when German pressure caused panic among Soviet units. (Novosti)

▶ Konstantin Konstantinovich Rokossovsky was commander of the Soviet Central Front and was tasked with containing Model's Ninth Army during the Kursk offensive. Afterwards he was commander of a number of Fronts until the end of the war. During the post-war period he became Deputy Minister of Defence, and was Inspector-General of the Ministry of Defence. Polish by birth, he was Poland's Minister of National Defence from 1949 to 1956. (Novosti)

THE OPPOSING COMMANDERS

The Soviet Commanders

In the wake of Stalingrad an enormous surge of confidence swept the Soviet Army. Notwithstanding the reverse at Kharkov in March, there was a very strong sense that not only had the tide turned against the German invader, but that victory was now certain. Such confidence was clearly manifest in the decision to engage the German Army in a deliberately defensive battle. By no means the least important factor in this resurgence of confidence was the emergence of a tier of senior officers, a new military élite, who had proven themselves in warfare.

Foremost amongst these was Georgi S. Zhukov, promoted to Marshal of the Soviet Union in January 1943, who could claim an unbroken series of victories to his credit, dating from the defeat of the Japanese Kwantung Army at Khalkin Gol in 1939. Having bested the Germans at Leningrad and in front of Moscow in 1941 and at Stalingrad in 1942, he now intended to do the same at Kursk. A taskmaster, he had an eye for military talent and under his tutelage a number of aspiring and promising generals, some to serve at Kursk, rapidly rose to the fore.

Of these, the most significant for our purposes were the troika of Vatutin, Rokossovsky and Konev. All three had participated in the heavy fighting in southern Russia in 1942. Like Stalin, Zhukov had a particularly high regard for the talents of Vatutin. He it was who forcibly argued the case for facing down the German offensive, in terms that later would be much more extensively reasoned by Zhukov himself. Rokossovsky was one of those rare birds in the Red Army, a senior officer who had survived three years in an NKVD prison during the purges. He was released in March 1940 in the wake of the Finland débâcle, albeit minus some teeth! His talents had been

noted by Stalin, who ordered his release. Seriously wounded during the Moscow counter-offensive, he did not return to active service until September 1942 when he assumed command of the Don Front. Ivan Konev, appointed to command the Steppe Military District in June 1943, was also a

▲ General of the Army Ivan Stepanovich Konev was appointed to command the Steppe Military District, renamed Steppe Front on 10 July 1943. He was responsible for the largest single reserve assembled by the Supreme Staff of the Staff Command (STAVKA) during the entire war. Throughout the remainder of the war he commanded a number of Fronts including 1st Ukrainian Front which captured Berlin. After the war he held numerous high military positions including Commander-in-Chief of the Soviet Union's Land Forces. (Novosti)

veteran of the first two years of the war. After Kursk, early in 1944, Vatutin was killed by Ukrainian nationalists; the other two were promoted, eventually becoming Marshals of the Soviet Union. It was against these 'new' men that the German Army would pit some its ablest 'sons'.

The German Commanders

The foremost German soldier involved in 'Citadel' was Field Marshal Erich von Manstein, regarded by many as the one of greatest strategists of the war. His credentials in armoured warfare were impeccable, having masterminded the plan for the invasion of France in 1940 and led the drive of LVI Panzer Corps during the opening stages of 'Barbarossa'. In July 1943 he was commander of Army Group South, having assumed that responsibility when it had been designated Army Group Don in November 1942. Although the genesis of 'Citadel' emerged from his own proposals to Hitler for the conduct of the summer campaign and was inspired by his own victory in the counteroffensive at Kharkov, he became increasingly sceptical of its success, as delay followed delay. Nevertheless, he was not as forthright as was Guderian in opposing the scheme, being as the latter observed, never at his best when faced by Hitler.

His partner in his labours on the southern sector of the salient was Hermann Hoth, commander of Fourth Panzer Army, a responsibility that he assumed in June 1942 and was to hold until dismissed by Hitler in November 1943. A highly experienced tank commander, having his own Panzer Group during 'Barbarossa', he took part in many of the great encirclement battles of 1941. Sharing many of von Manstein's doubts about 'Citadel', he nevertheless devoted much care to maximizing its chances of success, given the circumstances.

Ostensibly the commander of the northern attack on the salient, Field Marshal Günther von Kluge, took a back seat role to his subordinate, Walther Model, commanding general of Ninth Army. This was as much a reflection of his lack of enthusiasm for the offensive as it was of Hitler's faith in Model, though von Kluge's ambivalence

▲Colonel General Hermann Hoth was physically slight and silver haired, and affectionately known to his men as 'Papa Hoth'. Originally an infantryman, he had served on the Supreme General Staff during the First World War. He then served in the Reichswehr and in 1935 came the first in a rapid sequence of promotions. Switching from the infantry to the Panzertruppen, he commanded XV Panzer Corps in Poland. His Corps was the first to cross the Meuse during the invasion of France on 13 May 1940. During 'Barbarossa' he commanded Third Panzer Group of Army Group Centre. During the 1942 summer campaign he commanded Fourth Panzer Army until Hitler removed him in November 1943. (Bundesarchiv)

▶ *Field Marshal Günther von Kluge was the commander of Army Group Centre during Operation 'Citadel'. In 'Barbarossa' he commanded Fourth Army and was involved in the advance on Moscow. On 19 December 1941 he assumed command of Army Group Centre. A fractious relationship with Guderian that had developed in the wake of 'Barbarossa', came to a head as the Soviet counter-offensive before Moscow gathered pace.*

Von Kluge told Hitler that either he or Guderian, then commanding Second Panzer Army, must go. On 25 December Guderian was relieved of his command. Throughout 1942 and, in particular, the winter of 1942/3, Army Group Centre fought several severe defensive battles. Von Kluge committed suicide in August 1944, having been relieved of his command of the German forces in Normandy.
(Bundesarchiv)

when it came to openly expressing his doubts led to his position being regarded as two-faced. Model's rise had been prodigious. A divisional commander at the start of 'Barbarossa', his expertise in defensive warfare and his pro-Nazi stance brought him to Hitler's attention. In a very real sense 'Citadel' became Model's battle. His constant demand for more armour led to delay after delay as the strength of the Soviet defences became apparent. While Model's own strength did increase, it was in the end more than counterbalanced by the Soviet defensive preparations, which were on a scale never before experienced.

▶ *Colonel General Walther Model was a major-general in 1938. During 'Barbarossa' he commanded 3rd Panzer Division. His rise to fame followed his appointment to the command of Ninth Army on 12 January 1942. Throughout the winter he conducted a successful defence against Soviet forces attempting to capture Rzhev. His continued defence of this forward position throughout 1942 and his highly successful withdrawal of all German units from the Rzhev*

salient in Operation 'Buffalo' in March 1943 earned him a deserved reputation as a defensive specialist. After Kursk Hitler came to rely on Model's defensive skills more and more. He was appointed Field Marshal on 1 March 1944. Although referred to as 'the Führer's fireman' he was unable to prevent the Allied breakout from their Normandy bridgehead in August 1944. He committed suicide following the Battle of the Ruhr pocket in April 1945.
(Bundesarchiv)

ORDER OF BATTLE
GERMAN FORCES, I JULY 1943

ARMY GROUP CENTRE: Field Marshal von Kluge

9th ARMY: Col-Gen Model

XX Army Corps

Gen of the Inf Freiherr von Roman

45th Inf Div: Maj-Gen Freiherr von Falkenstein
72nd Inf Div: Lt-Gen Muller-Gebhard
137th Inf Div: Lt-Gen Kamecke
251st Inf Div: Maj-Gen Felzmann

XLVI Panzer Corps

Gen of the Inf Zorn

7th Inf Div: Lt-Gen von Rappard
31st Inf Div: Lt-Gen Hossbach
102nd Inf Div: Maj-Gen Hitzfeld
258th Inf Div: Lt-Gen Hocker

XLVII Panzer Corps

Gen of the PzTr Lemelsen

2nd Pz Div: Lt-Gen Lubbe
6th Inf Div: Lt-Gen Grossmann
9th Pz Div: Lt-Gen Scheller
20th Pz Div: Maj-Gen von Kessel

XLI Panzer Corps

Gen of the PzTr Harpe

18th Pz Div: Maj-Gen von Schlieben
86th Inf Div: Lt-Gen Weidling
292nd Inf Div: Lt-Gen von Kluge

XXIII Army Corps

Gen of the Inf Freissner

78th Sturm Div: Lt-Gen Traut
216th Inf Div: Maj-Gen Schack
383rd Inf Div: Maj-Gen Hoffmeister

Luftflotte Six

Col-Gen von Greim

1st Air Div: Lt-Gen Deichmann

ARMY GROUP SOUTH: Field Marshal von Manstein

ARMY DETACHMENT KEMPF:
Gen of the PzTr Kempf

4th PANZER ARMY:
Col-Gen Hoth

XI Army Corps

Gen of the PzTr Raus

106th Inf Div: Lt-Gen Forst
320th Inf Div: Maj-Gen Postel

XLII Army Corps

Gen of the Inf Mattenklott

39th Inf Div: Lt-Gen Loenweneck
161st Inf Div: Lt-Gen Recke
282nd Inf Div: Maj-Gen Kohler

II SS Panzer Corps

SS-Obergruppenführer Hausser

1st SS PzGren Div 'Leibstandarte Adolf Hitler':
  SS-Brigadeführer Wisch
2nd SS PzGren Div 'Das Reich':
  SS-Gruppenführer Kruger
3rd SS PzGren Div 'Totenkopf':
  SS-Brigadeführer Priess

III Panzer Corps

Gen of the PzTr Breith

6th Pz Div: Maj-Gen von Hunersdorff
7th Pz Div: Lt-Gen Freiherr von Funck
19th Pz Div: Lt-Gen G. Schmidt
168th Inf Div: Maj-Gen Chales de Beaulieu

XLVIII Panzer Corps

Gen of the PzTr von Knobelsdorff

3rd Pz Div: Lt-Gen Westhoven
11th Pz Div: Maj-Gen Mickl
167th Inf Div: Lt-Gen Trierenberg
PzGren Div 'Grossdeutschland':
  Lt-Gen Hoernlein

LII Army Corps

Gen of the Inf Ott

57th Inf Div: Maj-Gen Fretter-Pico
255th Inf Div: Lt-Gen Poppe
332nd Inf Div: Lt-Gen Schaefer

Luftflotte Four

Gen of the Luftwaffe Dessloch

THE OPPOSING ARMIES

The German Army

The lull in operations prior to the launch of 'Citadel' on 5 July, allowed the German forces earmarked for the operation to achieve a level of preparedness never before seen on the Eastern Front. But there were weaknesses in the order of battle which were to have a significant impact on the conduct of the operation.

The most important of these lay in the decline of the number of available infantry divisions and a reduction in their respective manpower strengths. The losses of the winter had resulted in infantry divisions being reduced from nine to six battalions. By 1943 the 17,734 men of the 1939 establishment had been reduced to 12,772. Despite their greater firepower, this shortage of infantry was to lead to panzer units being required to take upon themselves tasks normally the preserve of the infantry.

Nevertheless a total of 23 infantry divisions were earmarked for the offensive.

Hitler's continued commitment to 'Citadel' was ultimately grounded in his conviction that the

▼ *Designed and produced as a direct consequence of the Wehrmacht's encounter with the technically superior T-34 and KV-1 in the early days of 'Barbarossa', the Panther was expected to give the Germans the technical edge on the battlefield. It was well armoured, and armed with a very high-velocity gun that could defeat all known Soviet and Allied armour at long range. The expectation that its deployment in bulk by 10 Panzer Brigade would prove a battle winner during 'Citadel' was disappointed by bad luck and the fact that it was being committed to battle too soon; the brigade mechanics were still dealing with problems in the drive mechanism while the Panthers were entrained for the front. (Bundesarchiv)*

Weighed down by the bulk of the MG-42 and ammunition belts he is carrying, an infantryman of the 'Grossdeutschland' Division struggles forward in the initial German advance at Kursk. Of note is the distinctive 'GD' cuff band on the right sleeve and the monogrammed insignia on the shoulder-boards.

▶ *The 'Ferdinand' (from its designer, Dr Ferdinand Porsche) was a heavy tank destroyer. Built on the chassis of the failed Porsche design for the Tiger tank, ninety of these self-propelled 8.8cm PaK 43(L/71) anti-tank guns saw service at Kursk, exclusively with Ninth Army. This gun belonged to 3rd Company, Panzerjägerabteilung 654, commanded by Major Noak. The white 'N' used by the vehicles in his battalion can be seen on the frontal armour in front of the driver's position. (M. Jaugitz)*

sheer weight and momentum of the panzer divisions must carry the Germans to victory. Indeed, 'Citadel' witnessed the greatest assembly of German armour ever deployed for an offensive on such a limited front. Just two years before, Hitler had deployed 3,332 tanks to invade the Soviet Union along a total frontage of 930 miles. For 'Citadel' he would deploy 2,700 panzers and assault guns along a front just sixty miles wide and, for the first time since 'Barbarossa', the German Army would be fielding tanks superior to those of the Red Army. By dint of prodigious efforts on the production lines and by ruthlessly denuding other sectors, 63 per cent of all the 'battleworthy' panzers available on the Eastern Front were allocated to von Manstein and von Kluge. In addition to the 1,850 panzers, there were 533 assault guns and 200 obsolete panzers serving with the divisions. These machines were distributed among sixteen panzer and panzer grenadier divisions, and three assault gun brigades.

In theory a 1943 panzer division had a nominal strength of 15,600 men with from 150 to 200 machines, organized into a tank regiment of two or three battalions, a panzer grenadier brigade, an artillery regiment and divisional support units. In practice, however, there was great variation in divisional size and strength. At Kursk, the average actual strength of Army panzer divisions was just

73 machines. The strongest panzer units in the battle were the three Waffen SS panzer grenadier divisions of II SS Panzer Corps, and the élite Army panzer grenadier division 'Grossdeutschland'. On 5 July 'Leibstandarte Adolf Hitler', 'Das Reich' and 'Totenkopf' each deployed on average 131 panzers and 35 assault guns with 'Grossdeutschland' deploying 160 panzers and 35 assault guns. The bulk of the panzers at Kursk were late model Panzer IIIs and Panzer IVs, but it was to the triumvirate of Tiger 1 and Panther tanks and the Ferdinand self-propelled gun that Hitler looked to secure victory at Kursk. The Tiger had already acquired a formidable reputation on the Eastern front. Apart from the three Waffen SS divisions and 'Grossdeutschland', which had their own Tiger companies, all other tanks of this type were issued to the specially formed heavy tank battalions. These were allocated at army or corps level, and were sent to serve with other units as needs arose. The Panther was an unknown quantity, although much was expected of it. Designed in response to the superior T-34 and KV-1, it was to restore technical superiority to the *Panzerwaffe* in the East. On paper it could counter all known Soviet armour, but it was being committed to battle too early. Impatient to have this new vehicle for the offensive, Hitler ignored Guderian's protestations that it was being deployed before the

technical problems attending its introduction had been ironed out, but the start date of the offensive was delayed to ensure the Panther's employment. By 5 July sufficient Panthers were available to equip 1st Battalion 'Grossdeutschland' and two more Army battalions which together formed 10 Panzer Brigade with 200 of the type on strength. Some Panthers were also in operation with the Waffen SS divisions. A design of great potential, at Kursk it was prove a disappointment.

A similar tale of unrealized expectations attended the début of the Jagdpanzer Ferdinand committed to action with Ninth Army. Outwardly impressive, mounting a powerful 8.8cm gun, the machine was nevertheless castigated by Guderian as being excessively complex in design and for being devoid of even one machine-gun for close-in defence. Ninety were issued to the two battalions organized as Jagdpanzer Regiment 656. The turretless assault gun, being cheaper and easier to manufacture than a tank, was deployed in growing numbers. Although designed for infantry support, by 1943 it was serving principally as a tank destroyer. A total of 533 of them were integrated into the panzer divisions and independent assault gun brigades. Alongside them appeared a range of other vehicles, some of which were also making their combat début at Kursk. One of these was the 'Brummbär', a heavily armoured assault infantry gun mounted on a Panzer IV chassis and sporting a 15.cm howitzer. Sixty-six of these were issued to Sturmpanzerabteilung 216 attached to Model's Ninth Army. The 'Nashorn', mounting the PaK 43/1 (L/71) 8.8cm gun, and the 'Hummel' and

▲First deployed at Kursk, the 'Brummbär'(Grizzly Bear) was a heavily armoured SPG designed to destroy enemy fortifications. Mounting a 15.0cm Sturmhaubitze L/12 which fired a 38kg shell. Designed as a *consequence of the experience of street fighting in Stalingrad, it is seen here, in a rare picture, serving with Sturmpanzer Abteilung 216 of Ninth Army. (M. Jaugitz)*

'Wespe' self-propelled guns were also employed in large numbers for the first time.

The Luftwaffe

To support this mighty armoured phalanx, the Luftwaffe had assembled 1,800 aircraft, representing some two-thirds of all aircraft available in the east. In support of Ninth Army Luftflotte 4, had allocated 1st Luftwaffe Air Division, while the whole of Luftflotte 6 was available to support the southern thrust. On the crowded airfields around Orel, Belgorod and Kharkov were grouped the Heinkel He 111s and Junkers Ju 88s of KGs 3, 27 and 55; fighter units were drawn from JGs 3, 51, 52 and 54, flying Focke-Wulf Fw 190A-5s and Messerschmitt Bf 109G-6s. Although the Soviet Air force had made great strides, the Luftwaffe still held the edge, both in the quality of its fighters and the expertise of its pilots. Of particular importance, was the first deployment, *en masse*, of the Schlachtgeschwader units flying Fw 190s and Henschel Hs 129s. 'Citadel' also saw the last, widespread use of the *Stukagruppen* 'in the classic dive-bomber role.

▲The Henschel Hs 129B-2/R2s ground-attack/anti-tank aircraft of Schlachtgeschwader 1 were to see extensive service in support of the operations of Fourth Panzer Army. The armament of this variant is clearly seen here. In the nose are two 7.92mm machine-guns and two 20mm cannon. More significant, however, was the 30mm Mk 101 cannon mounted in the gondola beneath the fuselage. In combination with other ground-attack types, the Henschel was to cause the Soviets problems, particularly during the early and 'rapid' advance of the SS Panzer Corps. (Bundesarchiv)

▼ 'Citadel' saw the last widespread use of the legendary Stuka in the classic dive-bombing role. Experience had long shown that the Stuka could only function effectively where the Luftwaffe could maintain air superiority. At Kursk, however, Soviet air power was very much stronger and the slow Ju-87 became a sitting duck for fighters, large numbers being lost in the course of the battle. After 'Citadel' the dive-bomber role was rescinded and all the Stukas were transferred to Schlactgeschwaders (ground-attack wings) for low-level ground attack. (Bundesarchiv)

GERMAN ARMOUR

Panzer strength during Operation 'Citadel'. This table is based on divisional strength returns and so cannot be taken as definitive of the actual strength of the divisions involved.

	Panzerkampfwagen:			Other
	VI	IV/V	III	types
Army Group Centre				
Ninth Army:				
2nd Panzer Div		60	38	38 old[1]
4th Panzer Div		52	40	16 old[1]
9th Panzer Div		64	30	17 old[1]
12th Panzer Div		35	20	30 old[1]
18th Panzer Div		20	12	43 old[1]
20th Panzer Div		40	20	25 old[1]
21 Panzer Bde				
216th Panzer Bn				66 'Brumm-bär'[2]
505th Panzer Bn		45[3]		8 *Obs*
656th PzJäg Reg				
653 PzJäg Bn				45 Ferdinand, 10[1] old[1]
654 PzJäg Bn		5		45 Ferdinand, 5[1] old[1]
Assault Gun Bns: 177, 185, 189, 244, 245, 904, 909				250 Stug IIIs

Second Army: SP anti-tank Bns: 202, 559, 616
100 AGs and ATs

Army Group South				
Fourth Panzer Army:				
3rd Pz Div			33	30	2 AGs, 39 old[1]
11th Pz Div			48	50	20 old, 3 *Flam*
'GD' Pz Gren Div	14	100	20	35 AGs, 12 old[1]
				14 *Flam*
1st SS Pz Gren Div	13	85	12	35 AGs, 7 old[1]
2nd SS Pz Gren Div	14	68	46	34 AGs, 1 old[1]
3rd SS Pz Gren Div	15	78	47	35 AGs, 8 old[1]

10 Panzer Brigade				
51st Pz Bn		100		Panthers
52nd Pz Bn		100		Panthers
911th Assault Gun Bn				31 AGs
Army Group Kempf:				
503rd Pz Bn	48			Tiger I
6th Pz Div		53	33	25 old[1], 13 Flam
7th Pz Div		46	41	16 old[1]
19th Pz Div		48	22	12 old[1]
Assault Gun Brigades: 228, 393, 905				75 AGs

XXIV Panzer Corps (Army Group South Reserve for 'Citadel')

5th SS Pz Gren Div		20	11	6 AGs, 15 old
23rd Pz Div		40	21	11 old

Key:
[1] Earlier models of panzers still operated by the division, e.g., Pz 38(t) and Panzer II. Also includes marks of Panzer III and IV equipped with 3.7cm, short 5.0cm and 7.5cm guns.
[2] Sturmpanzer 'Brummbär' (Grizzly Bear); 66 were employed for the first time at Kursk by 216th Panzer (Sturm) Battalion.
[3] Only 1st and 2nd Companies of sPzAbt 505 available at the onset of 'Citadel'. 3rd Company not committed until 8 July.
AG Assault Gun.
AT Self-propelled anti-tank weapons; armament either 7.5cm PaK 40 as in Marder II, III or the 8.8cm PaK 43/1 mounted on the Gw III/IV 'Hornisse' as used during 'Citadel'.
Flam Flame-thrower Panzer III Ausf 'M'.
Obs Observation

Of the Tiger Is, PzKpfw Vs, IVs and IIIs employed during 'Citadel', 15, 110 and 80 respectively were command tanks (Befehlswagen). In all, 60 flame-thrower Mark IIIs were used in the offensive.

INFANTRY GUNS AND HEAVY ARTILLERY

	Weight of Shell	Weight in Action	Range		Weight of Shell	Weight in Action	Range
German				**Soviet**			
105cm lFH18	14.8kg	1,958kg	10,675m	762mm Type 39	6.35kg	780kg	8,504m
15.0cm sIG23	38kg	1,700kg	4,700m	122mm Type 31/37	22.5kg (HE)	7,117kg	20.8km
15.0cm sFH18	43.5kg	5,512kg	13,250m	152mm M-1937	43.6kg	7,128kg	17.265km

Panzer III. Along with Panzer IV, the Panzer III provided the bulk of the armour the Germans employed during 'Citadel'. By the summer of 1943, however, its days as a battle tank were numbered. As with the Panzer IV, remedial action

in the form of upgunning and uparmouring had effected a partial redress

in its technical inferiority compared with the T-34. Unlike the Panzer IV, its smaller size meant that its turret ring could not accommodate the long-barrelled high-velocity 75mm gun now needed to

deal with Soviet armour. The Model M illustrated here carried the 50mm L/60 and schurzen and was equipped for deep wading. Losses at Kursk were high. Production of the Panzer III ended in August 1943.

The Soviet Army

Even as the German Army began its numerical and qualitative decline, the Soviet Army was evolving into an organization totally unlike that of even a year before. The re-introduction of uniform insignia, the designating of certain units as 'Guards' formations in the Tsarist fashion, imparted to the Red Army a sense of its own destiny that had profound psychological benefits to its collective sense of purpose. During the first two years of warfare they had received harsh and terrible lessons that even now were still being assimilated. But a growing sense of professionalism was pervading the army, that was of itself to have a profound impact on the result of the coming battle. Political slogans were eschewed as being no substitute for knowledge of the 'art of war'. It was certainly no longer the case that the Germans could depict the Red Army as merely a rabble of uniformed peasants.

Upsurge in morale was matched by the increasing size and strength of the army. As the Germans wrestled with the problem of declining

ORDER OF BATTLE: SOVIET FORCES, 1 JULY 1943

STALIN

STAVKA

Stavka Representatives for Battle of Kursk:
Marshal Zhukov and Marshal Vasilevsky

Central Front	Steppe (Reserve) Front	Voronezh Front
Gen of the Army K. R. Rokossovsky	**Col-Gen I. S. Konev**	**Gen of the Army N. F. Vatutin**
48th Army: Lt-Gen Romanenko	5th Guards Army: Lt-Gen Zhadov	38th Army: Lt-Gen Moskalenko
13th Army: Lt-Gen Pukhov	5th Guards Tank Army: Lt-Gen Rotmistrov	40th Army: Lt-Gen Moskalenko
70th Army: Lt-Gen Galanin	27th Army: Lt-Gen Trofimenko	1st Tank Army: Lt-Gen Katukov
65th Army: Lt-Gen Batov	47th Army: Lt-Gen Ryzhov	6th Guards Army: Lt-Gen Chistyakov
60th Army: Lt-Gen Chernyahovsky	53rd Army: Lt-Gen Mangarov	7th Guards Army: Lt-Gen Shumilov
2nd Tank Army: Lt-Gen Rodin	5th Air Army: Col-Gen Goryunov	
16th Air Army: Air Marshal Rudenko		2nd Air Army: Air Marshal Krasovski

manpower, Soviet Army numbers had never been higher. At the beginning of July a total of 16,442,000 officers and men were under arms. While equipment levels were impressively high they could also be misleading. Of the 9,918 tanks in service, nearly one-third were light tanks, of dubious value on the modern battlefield. In artillery, more than 50 per cent of the 103,085 guns and mortars were the less effective 7.6cm and 8.2cm calibres. Both areas were to see major shifts towards the production of large numbers of technically superior weapons.

Soviet tank production had been ruthlessly restricted to a few models since the beginning of the war. Updating designs, such as that of the T-34, had been deliberately avoided so as to maintain continuity and hence volume of output. But rumours of new German designs and the capture of the first Tiger in December 1942 shook up the Commissariat for Tank Production. The decision to revamp the T-34 with a new, 8.5cm gun was initiated, but the model was too late to see service at Kursk. The new SU-85 tank destroyer was also too late for the battle. The hastily developed SU-152 was employed, in limited numbers but with devastating effect. Nevertheless

the Soviet Army won the tank battles at Kursk even though, for the first time since 1941, the Germans were fielding qualitatively superior machines.

But the greatest killer of German armour and troops was the Soviets' 'Queen of the battlefield', the artillery, deployed in unprecedented numbers during the battle. Anti-tank guns were organized into brigades, as were the howitzers of 152mm and

ASSAULT GUNS/ TANK DESTROYERS

	Armour	Gun (mph)	Speed (tons)	Weight
German	(front/ side)			
Sturmgeschütz III G	80/30mm	7.5cm Stuk 40 L/48	25	23.9
Jagdpanzer 'Ferdinand'	100/80mm	8.8cm PaK 43/2 L/71	12.5	65
Panzerjäger Hornisse, 'Nashorn'	30/20/10	8.8cm PaK 43/2 L/71	25	25
Soviet				
SU-76	35/16	76.2mm ZIS-3	30	11.2
SU-122	45/45	122mm M-30S	31	30.9
SU-152	60/60	152mm ML-20S	29	45.5

TANKS

	Armour (front/ side)	Main Gun	Speed (mph)	Weight (tons)
German				
Panzer III Ausf M	50/30mm	5.0cm KwK39 L/60	25	22.3
Panzer IV Ausf H	80/30mm	7.5cm KwK40 L/48	25	23.5
Panzer V Ausf D Panther	100/45mm	7.5cm KwK42 L/70	34	43
Panzer VI Ausf E Tiger	100/60mm	8.8cm KwK36 L/56	23	56
Soviet				
T-34 Model 43	47/60mm	76.2mm F-34	31	30.9
KV-1 Model 41	75/75mm	76.2mm F-34	35	45
Churchill Mk III	88/76mm	57mm	15.5	39
M3 'Lee'	50/38mm	75/37mm	26	
T-70	45/45	45mm	32	9.2

ANTI-TANK GUNS

	Weight of Shell (lb)	Muzzle Velocity (fps)	Penetration
German			
5.0cm PaK38	1.81[1]	3,925	120mm at 500m
7.5cm PaK40	7.04[1]	3,250	154mm at 500m
8.8cm FlaK 37	20.25	2,690	90mm at 2,030m
Soviet			
4.5cm Model 42	1.09[1]	3,500	54mm at 500m
5.7cm Model	3.8[1]	4,200	100mm at 500m

[1]indicates weight of tungsten-cored ammunition.

203mm calibre. In late 1942 sixteen of the twenty-six artillery divisions were organized as 'breakthrough divisions' deploying an unprecedented 356 guns in their firing line. Other permutations on the mass fire theme, such as the 'artillery breakthrough corps' and the Katyusha divisions, were introduced.

In mobility and in the air the Soviet Army also began to see significant changes. The influx of 183,000 Lend Lease lorries by mid-1943 went some way to imparting mobility to some of the major units but demand always outstripped supply. In the air new fighters such as the Yakovlev Yak-9D and the Lavochkin La-5FN began to appear in large numbers, as did the improved Ilyushin Il-2m3 mounting a 37mm anti-tank cannon that was to wreak so much havoc amongst German armour during the battle. In terms of quality and quantity the Luftwaffe was finding matters more difficult in the air on the Eastern front, to the unhappiness of the ground units.

Whereas there is a strong sense that the Wehrmacht had not perceived this fundamental and continuing qualitative change in the Soviet Army by the beginning of 'Citadel', they were always conscious of Soviet quantitative superiority. While in many areas the Soviet Army had yet to match the sophistication of the Wehrmacht, there is no doubting that the Red Army of 1943 was a very different animal from that of June 1941.

FIGHTER AIRCRAFT

	Speed	Ceiling	Range	Armament
German				
Messerschmitt Bf 109G-6	428	38,000	365/460	one 30mm Mk 108 two 13mm MG 131 (plus two 20mm MG 151 in underwing gondolas)
Focke-Wulf Fw 190	408	37,400	560	two 20mm cannon, two MG 131, two MG 151
Soviet				
Lavochkin La5FN	403	20,670	475	two 20mm cannon
Yakovlev Yak-3	403	35,500	450	one 20mm cannon, two 12.7 MG

BOMBERS

	Max speed (mph)	Ceiling (ft)	Bomb (lb)	Range (miles)
German				
Heinkel He111	258	25,950	4,410	745
Heinkel He177	295	26,500	13,200	3,000
Junkers Ju 88	269	26,900	6,614	1,112
Soviet				
Petlyakov Pe-2	281	28,870	2,204	817
Petlyakov Pe-8	212	26,900	8,818	2,113
Ilyushin DB-3F	208	28,545	5,952	2,360

GROUND-ATTACK AND DIVE-BOMBER AIRCRAFT

	Max speed (mph)	Ceiling (ft)	Bomb (lb)	Range (miles)		Max speed (mph)	Ceiling (ft)	Bomb (lb)	Range (miles)
German					**Soviet**				
Junkers Ju 87D	242	24,000	3,968	373	Ilyushin Il-2m3	251	19,500	1,321[2]	375
Henschel Hs129B	253	29,530	220[1]	547					

[1]The version employed at Kursk was the R2 model armed with a 30mm Mk 103 cannon in a gondola beneath the fuselage.
[2]The Il-2m3 also carried two N-37 or P-37 anti-tank cannon, two ShKAS 7.62mm machine-guns and one rearward-facing B.S. 12,7mm machine-gun in the rear cockpit.

Responsible for the destruction of many German panzers in the entrenched defences of the Kursk salient were Soviet infantry platoons employing the PTRD or PTRS anti-tank rifles. The figure shown here is wearing the new 1943 regulation 'gymnastiorka' and shoulder-boards.

PLANS AND PREPARATIONS

It was not until 1 July that Hitler told his senior Eastern Front commanders that he intended to launch 'Citadel' on the 5th. The die was now irrevocably cast, yet throughout the months of vacillation and delay, despite irrefutable evidence that the Soviets had transformed the salient into an enormous defensive bastion, no substantive attempt had been made to alter the plans for the offensive. Although the design for 'Citadel' remained as set forth in Operation Order No. 6, the conditions and rationale that had given rise to the OKH plan in April had long ceased to have any validity. Only in the build-up of the immense German forces, over and above those originally envisaged as being necessary for 'Citadel', was there any suggestion that account had been taken of the true situation. Despite the strenuous and ingenious attempts they employed to disguise their intentions, the build-up of German forces on each side of the neck of the Kursk salient was on such a scale that it was impossible for the enemy not to know what was coming. Strategic surprise was dead. Within twenty-four hours of the conference at the Wolfsschanze, Stalin was able (courtesy of intelligence from 'Lucy') to inform the commanders of the Voronezh, Central and Steppe Fronts that the Germans would go over to the offensive between 3 and 6 July. All the Germans could hope for now was that they could achieve tactical surprise in terms of choosing the time, place and main weight of the attack, and the method to be employed.

The German Plans

The OKH plan for 'Citadel' provided for a concentric attack by units of Army Groups Centre and South against Kursk. The aims of the offensive were simply stated – to seal off the Kursk salient along the line Maloarkhangelsk–Kursk–Belgorod and bring to battle and destroy the very strong Soviet forces therein. By July the forces thought adequate to achieve this end had been assembled. The final disposition of German units and their specific attack objectives on the eve of the offensive were as follows.

Units of Army Group Centre, operating as Ninth Army, were to break through the Soviet defences along a line between the Kursk–Orel highway and railway and then drive southwards to Kursk. In addition OKH had tasked Ninth Army with pushing the front line eastwards as far as Maloarkhangelsk, to establish continuity with the right wing of Second Panzer Army. To achieve these objectives Ninth Army had been allocated V Corps Headquarters with fifteen infantry divisions and seven panzer and panzer grenadier divisions.

The units of Army Group South earmarked for 'Citadel' were divided between Fourth Panzer Army and Army Detachment 'Kempf'. Hermann Hoth, commander of Fourth Panzer Army, had been allocated 'Grossdeutschland' Division, II SS Panzer Corps, five panzer divisions, 10 Panzer (Panther) Brigade and two infantry divisions, making it the most powerful armoured formation ever assembled for an offensive under a single commander in the history of the German Army. This immense phalanx of armour was tasked with crashing through the Soviet defences along a thirty-mile front, between Belgorod and Gertsovka, and driving a wedge through to the town of Oboyan and thence to Kursk. A vigorous flank cover for the thrust by Fourth Panzer Army would be provided by the units of Army Detachment 'Kempf'. Driving northwards, they would meet units of Ninth Army, at a point to the east of Kursk, in order to establish the new front line. This secondary attack, between Belgorod and Korocha, was to be launched on a front of just fifteen miles. Total forces allocated to Army

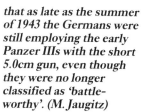

▲ *During the weeks before 'Citadel' both sides trained hard for the coming offensive. Here 'Ferdinands' of Panzer-jägerabteilung 654* exercise with Panzer IIIs of its associated 'Goliath' demolition unit. Packed with explosives, this small tracked vehicle was 'launched', under radio control from the Mark III, into the Soviet minefields where they were then detonated to clear a path for the Ferdinands. The photograph also shows *that as late as the summer of 1943 the Germans were still employing the early Panzer IIIs with the short 5.0cm gun, even though they were no longer classified as 'battle-worthy'. (M. Jaugitz)*

◄ *General of Panzer Troops Werner Kempf's three corps had the difficult task of screening the eastern flank of the northwards moving II SS Panzer Corps. As happened to all the major German formations involved in the offensive, his planned rate of advance fell off sharply in the face of the powerful Soviet defences and the difficult terrain his panzer divisions encountered east of the River Donets. (Bundesarchiv)*

Group South constituted V Corps Headquarters with nine panzer and panzer grenadier divisions, and eight infantry divisions.

For some months before 'Citadel' the Luftwaffe had been raiding Soviet airfields, railways, roads and troop concentrations within the salient, and in 'strategic' attacks on industrial targets beyond the Urals. On the tactical level, an integral and crucial element in the success of the ground offensive was the requirement that the Luftwaffe secure air superiority over the battlefield. This was essential, not only to prevent the panzer columns being attacked from the air, but also to give protection to the now very vulnerable 'Stukagruppen'. The latter had a very important role in the battle, functioning as flying artillery, to compensate the Germans' shortage in that arm. The deployment of the specialized ground attack units *en masse* for the first time was also expected to make a significant contribution to the success of the offensive.

As the German formations moved to their start positions on the two nights preceding the attack, their respective dispositions revealed much about the different approaches, taken by Model and von Manstein, to the task of cracking the formidable Soviet defences. Ninth Army was drawn up in a deeply echeloned formation along a frontage of forty miles. The offensive would open with an attack by nine infantry divisions with their own organic assault gun units, but supported by only one panzer division. Model had decided to hold the bulk of his armour in reserve until the infantry had prized open the defences, whereupon the panzers would be released to drive through the gaps, turn the Soviet flanks and thrust to the rear. Von Manstein, on the other hand, had decided that his weakness in infantry precluded this approach. His trump card was the 700 panzers available to Fourth Panzer Army, which he was determined to employ from the outset, *en masse*, as a *Panzerkeil* or armoured wedge against the Soviet defences. To ensure the necessary critical mass, the breakthrough sectors for the assault had been reduced to 2.8–3.3 kilometres per division with an allocation of thirty to forty tanks per kilometre of front. He believed that such a concentration of armour would rapidly take the

German forces through the enemy defence lines and allow the panzer divisions to take on the Soviet armoured reserves in the open country beyond. To maintain the necessary momentum, the tank crews were ordered not to stop and recover damaged tanks. The crews in these tanks were to maintain fire from static positions. Such an order, in the light of the density of the Soviet anti-tank defences, was a death warrant. Von Manstein's expectations were not realized because of the great *matériel* superiority of the Red Army and the strength of the Soviet defences in the Kursk salient, the immensity of which had no parallel in history.

The Soviet Plans

By the end of May the Soviet strategy for the summer campaign and the preparations to meet the German offensive were complete. Having ground down the German armour in the defences of the salient, the Voronezh, Central, Steppe and Bryansk Fronts together with the right wing of the South-West and the left wing of the West Fronts were to go over to the counter-offensive. In the north and south, other Fronts acting in concert would also launch offensives, to pin down German forces as the major Soviet effort unfolded in the westwards drive to the Dnieper.

The Russians thought that the primary German blow would fall on the north-eastern sector of the salient. Rokossovsky, therefore, had massed the main strength of his Central Front along a 50-mile stretch, straddling what he thought would be the German thrust line to Kursk. Three of his five armies, 70th, 13th and 48th, were deployed to cover this sector. As 13th Army was expected to bear the brunt of the German attack, Rokossovsky had deployed 60 per cent of his artillery brigades and 33 per cent of his armour to support its operations. To the rear, 2nd Tank Army was deployed as the echelon reserve, and in general reserve he could call on a cavalry corps, two tank corps and several tank destroyer units. To provide air cover and support, STAVKA had allocated 16th Air Army. This concentration of forces gave Rokossovsky 2.1 superiority in artillery and 7.6 superiority in armour. In the south, Vatutin's

Tiger 1. The Tiger illustrated here belongs to the 2nd SS Panzer Grenadier Division 'Das Reich'. The fourteen Tigers available to the division for 'Citadel' formed the 8th company of the Panzer Regiment and could be identified by the 'white gnome' on the turret next to the vehicle code 'S13'. The 'S' designated a heavy panzer and the '13' placed it as the third vehicle of four in the first platoon. The special Kursk sign employed by 'Das Reich' of a horizontal bar with two vertical bars above is carried on the left glacis. The tanks of the 19th Panzer Division carried the same marking but in black – an attempt to confuse Soviet intelligence as to unit identity.

Voronezh Front was also able to deploy five armies, one tank army and an air fleet. He had deployed the bulk of his forces to cover the sectors he believed most likely to be attacked by von Manstein's forces, those corresponding to the centre and left of his 60-mile front. On the right he had deployed 6th Guards Army in echelon, to cover the approaches to Oboyan. From his knowledge of the OKH plan he assumed that the main weight of the German offensive would be along this axis, it being the shortest route·to Kursk. On the left he had deployed 7th Guards Army. To their rear was 1st Tank Army, tasked with covering the Oboyan/Kursk approach. Front reserves included three corps, 35th Guards Rifle Division and 5th Guards Tank Corps. While Vatutin could command a 2.1 superiority in artillery, in armour he was a little weaker than the German forces opposing him. During the course of the coming battle, however, it would become apparent that he had diluted his strength by spreading his forces over too wide a frontage. This would 'aid' the Germans in allowing them to achieve a much deeper penetration in the south of the salient than was achieved by Ninth Army. Nevertheless, to his rear, lay a complete reserve Front, on which he could call, mustering forces equal to one German panzer and three infantry corps plus smaller units.

Designated the Steppe Front, and commanded by General Konev, this was the largest strategic reserve assembled by STAVKA throughout the war, and its availability would ensure the German defeat. This huge force amounted to no fewer than five infantry armies, one tank army, one air army and six, including two armoured, reserve corps. In theory, it functioned as a screening force to block any German drive eastward should 'Citadel', in spite of everything, succeed. Zhukov, however, was more than confident that such an eventuality was unlikely, and that his principle objective – the destruction of the German armour – would be accomplished amidst the labyrinthine defence system of the salient itself.

The Soviet Defences

Following the decision of 12 April, the Soviet Army began to mobilize the civilian population to help prepare the defences. By the end of the month more than 105,000 civilians were at work, that figure rising to 300,000 by June. The object of their labours was the construction of a series of defences designed specifically to embroil, channel and 'bleed white' the mass of armour that the Germans were expected to deploy. Under the guidance of army engineers, a 'belt' of battalion fire and support positions, anti-tank 'resistance points' and mines linked by an extensive trench system was established. 8.5cm anti-aircraft guns and 12.2cm and 15.2cm howitzers supported by 12.0cm heavy mortars were emplaced in heavily camouflaged circular fire positions to bring rapid and very heavy fire to bear on the expected axes of the German advance. Anti-tank defence was centred on the 'resistance points', each containing an average of three to five 7.6cm anti-tank guns, troops equipped with anti-tank rifles and mortars, and sections of machine-gunners and sappers. These were laid out in chequer-board style, each strongpoint supporting another. The troops in these 'bunkers' had been given extensive training to deal with the panzers. In areas of particular vulnerability, up to twelve anti-tank guns, arranged as 'pakfronts', were emplaced in well-camouflaged positions from which they could level fire, *en masse*, against German armour, channelled towards them by carefully laid minefields. In total, the Soviets poured in more than 20,000 guns and mortars, 6,000 anti-tank guns and 920 Katyusha rocket batteries, to support the defences of the Central and Voronezh Fronts. During the spring the Red Army had laid more than 40,000 mines over the entire salient, in fields of wheat and sunflowers which, by high summer, rendered their presence invisible. The density of the minefields, particularly between the strongpoints, was remarkably high, with anti-tank mines averaging 2,400 per mile and anti-personnel mines 2,700 per mile. Trenches linking the strongpoints were dug on a vast scale with a total length for those in the salient approaching 3,100 miles.

The depth of these defences was staggering: eight defensive belts with a total depth of nearly 110 miles. These were reinforced to their rear, by the Steppe Front and a further defensive belt lay beyond that, covering the east bank of the River Don. But the Soviets certainly had no intention of receiving the German onslaught passively. Within the defences on each of the 'fronts', an army of several armoured corps was so disposed as to be able to counter-attack the German forces once their axes of advance became clear.

The immensity of the preparations and the scale of the forces being deployed left the soldiers of each side in no doubt as to the significance of the coming battle. Even Hitler, who was prepared to gamble all on this one throw though the very thought of it 'turned my stomach', said as much in his personal message to his soldiers: 'This day you are to take part in an offensive of such importance that the whole future of the war may depend on its outcome.'

▲Air power played a vital role at Kursk, with both sides employing very large numbers of aircraft. The Petlyakov Pe-2, a very versatile Soviet dive-bomber, was one of the main types employed for attacks on supply lines.

The ability of the Red Air Force to range far and wide in the rear of the German front line was to cause Ninth Army problems throughout the battle. (Novosti)

▼A German 15.0cm sFH 18 gun firing on Soviet positions at the start of Ninth Army's offensive against the Soviet Central Front. The Germans suffered a marked inferiority in heavy artillery compared to the Russians, so many guns having been lost in the 1942 campaign and at Stalingrad. It was for this reason that the Stukagruppen were to play such an important, if costly, role during the battle. (Bundesarchiv)

THE BATTLE OF KURSK

Forewarned that the Germans would go over to the offensive, between 3 and 6 July, Rokossovsky and Vatutin put their Fronts on full alert. In an atmosphere of high tension the soldiers stood to their weapons. Ammunition stocks were checked, weapons examined, maps pored over. For the last time, officers took their men through the methods learnt for stalking the panzers. Like a litany, the weak points of the Tiger were recited. Khrushchev's demand that they be known as well as the 'Lord's Prayer was once known', was more than adequately fulfilled. The heightened sense of anticipation was rendered the more uncomfortable by the heavy, sultry heat which hung like a pall over the whole region, relieved only by the warm rain of a summer thunderstorm. The past few days had seen intense aerial activity as both the Luftwaffe and Soviet Air Force bombed airfields and hit each other's lines of supply and communication. All the signs pointed to the imminence of the German offensive. As the hours ticked by, the two Front commanders demanded every iota of Intelligence that might indicate when precisely the Germans would attack. 'Lucy' had been unable to specify the exact hour of the start of 'Citadel', so a heightened vigilance was now being exercised by the front-line units, who had been warned to look especially for mine clearing parties operating in no-man's land.

5 July: Ninth Army/Central Front

Late in the evening of 4 July Rokossovsky obtained what he needed. A patrol had come across a team of German sappers clearing a Soviet minefield. Under interrogation the one prisoner taken said much about the German preparations for the offensive and revealed that it would begin at 0330 hours the following morning. Rokossovsky gave orders for the artillery, mortars and Katyusha units

in 13th Army sector to open fire on the German positions, which they did at 0220 hours.

To the still assembling German units, this completely unexpected hurricane of Soviet fire raised the disturbing possibility that the barrage was the prelude to a pre-emptive Soviet offensive. For more than half an hour the Soviet guns ranged across the German lines, causing considerable disruption in the assembly positions and delaying the Germans' attack for an hour.

At 0430 the German artillery opened up against the Soviet positions and by 0500 the forward observers of 13th Army reported heavy attacks against their front, supported by panzers and assault guns. Overhead, Stukas peeled off, plummeting earthward with sirens screaming, to drop their bombs on the known Russian defensive positions. By 0530 the German infantry had been committed along the 25-mile front of 13th Army and the right wing of 70th Army. Within an hour the strength of the Soviet defences had become apparent and the battle had already begun to assume the features that would characterize its savage course during the next nine days. The infantry, crossing open ground, were continually bombarded with artillery and mortars and subjected to intense small-arms fire from dug-in Soviet infantry. Attempts to use dead ground or the tall rye as cover resulted in casualties from the liberally sown anti-personnel mines. Losses began to mount steeply as the German troops finally made the first line of Soviet trenches only to find that their artillery had not been successful in destroying the enemy infantry; savage hand-to-hand fighting ensued. After a day-long struggle the German 258th Infantry Division, tasked with breaking through to the Kursk–Orel highway, had ground to a halt in the face of this unparalleled resistance, as had the 7th Infantry Division.

The Offensive of Model's Ninth Army, 5-11 July 1943

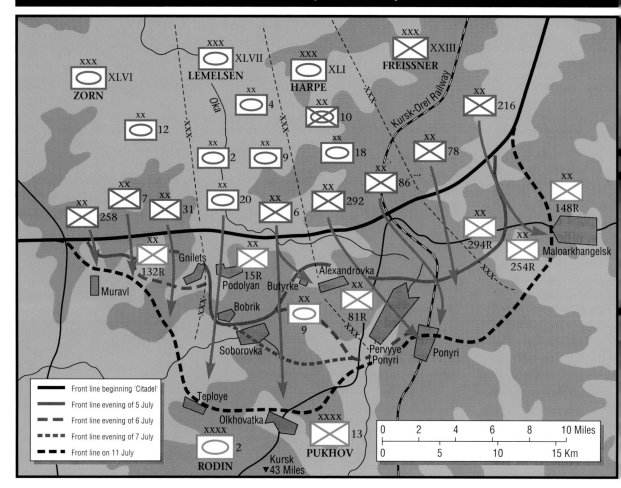

Legend:
- Front line beginning 'Citadel'
- Front line evening of 5 July
- Front line evening of 6 July
- Front line evening of 7 July
- Front line on 11 July

Map labels: ZORN XLVI, LEMELSEN XLVII, Oka, 12, 4, HARPE XLI, 10, FREISSNER XXIII, 216, 78, 86, Kursk-Orel Railway, 2, 9, 18, 148R, 7, 31, 20, 6, 292, 294R, 254R, Maloarkhangelsk, 258, 132R, Gnilets, 15R Podolyan, Butyrke, Alexandrovka, Muravl, Bobrik, 81R, 9, Pervyye Ponyri, Ponyri, Soborovka, Teploye, Olkhovatka, RODIN 2, PUKHOV 13, Kursk ▼43 Miles

0 2 4 6 8 10 Miles
0 5 10 15 Km

Greater success attended those infantry divisions that attacked with panzer support and these were concentrated on the 10-mile section of the front that corresponded to the main thrust line of Ninth Army. Of the six panzer divisions available to Model, only the 20th, was committed in the first wave of the attack. Engineers had to clear lanes through the minefields before its panzers could begin the assault. The first trench lines were breached and by 0900 the division's panzer Mark IIIs and IVs were deploying between the villages of Gnilets and Bobrik. Information from a prisoner that suggested a weak link in the Soviet defences led the divisional commander, General von Kessel, to order an attack on the village of Bobrik. Assisted by a heavy barrage from its divisional artillery and air support, 20th Panzer Division rolled up the

▲The Offensive of Model's Ninth Army, 5-11 July 1943 For six days the assembled might of Colonel General Model's Ninth Army was thrown against the defence lines of the Soviet forces in the north of the salient. Unlike his compatriot to the south, General Rokossovsky had concentrated his forces along a very much narrower front that corresponded to what he believed to be the main German axis of attack on Kursk. To some extent he was assisted in this by the stronger forces available to him, which arose from *the mistaken perception that it was the German northern thrust that was the stronger of the two. Nevertheless, after six days of bitter and ferocious combat the offensive strength of Ninth Army was spent. With all reserve forces committed by July, the Germans were ill-prepared to respond to the massive Soviet offensive that opened against Second Panzer Army and to the rear of Ninth Army on 12 July.*

▲ At Kursk 20th Panzer Division and others were able to employ their own organic panzer artillery in the form of the 'Hummel'. This self-propelled 15.0cm sFH 18 howitzer provided the panzer divisions with readily available artillery support when needed. Many 'Hummel' units had attached Panzer IIs, now obsolete as tanks, equipped with radios as command vehicles. (Bundesarchiv)

▼ Panzerkampfwagen III Ausf Ms, with their 'schurzen' side armour, of 20th Panzer Division deploy for battle. The thin 5mm armour provided a limited 'stand off' protection against the hollow charge anti-tank rounds the Soviets had introduced during the course of 1943. The tracks of the panzers leave wide swathes in the rye and cornfields, so much a feature of this sector of the front. It was among these fields that the Soviets had planted many thousands of mines. (Bundesarchiv)

◀ A 'Ferdinand' of Panzerjägerabteilung 653 and a supporting Panzer III attack the Soviet lines on 5 July. Once committed, the weakness of this machine was immediately apparent. While its very heavy armour carried it through the Russian positions with ease, once within the defence lines its vulnerability became all too obvious. Lacking a machine-gun, its ability to defend itself was confined to its huge 8.8cm PaK 43, which used against Soviet infantry, now trained to control their 'tank fright', was likened by Guderian to 'quail shooting with a cannon'. In its role as a long-range tank destroyer the 'Ferdinand' achieved success, but at Kursk it was to prove a failure. (M. Jaugitz)

front of 321st Rifle Regiment. In seizing Bobrik, the Germans had cracked the defensive positions of 15th Rifle Division and had advanced some three miles into the Soviet positions.

The Germans were under incessant air attack from 16th Air Army which was vigorously challenging German local air superiority over the battlefield. On the right of 20th Panzer, 6th Infantry Division had gone into action at 0620 and had thrust along the valley of the Oka. Some three hours later 1st and 2nd Companies of Heavy Panzer Battalion 505, equipped with Tiger Is and attached to 6th Infantry Division, moved forward. Advancing rapidly, the two Tiger regiments destroyed a defensive screen of T-34s and anti-tank guns before ploughing into the open flank of 676th Rifle Regiment. By midday Major Sauvant's Tigers had taken the village of Butyrki, threatening to unhinge the left wing of 81st Rifle Division which was already under pressure from 292nd Division of General Harpe's XLI Panzer Corps. This Soviet division had been fighting a savage battle throughout the morning. Penetrations of Soviet positions in this sector of 13th Army had been achieved by the Ferdinands of Jagdpanzer

Abteilung 653. While the detachment of Ferdinands operating with 292nd Infantry Division succeeded in driving straight through the defence lines of 81st Rifle Division to Alexsandrovka, their success was more apparent than real. Behind them the Soviet infantry sealed the breach, forcing the German infantry, now denuded of armour support, to fight for every yard.

Throughout the day, as pressure mounted on 13th Army, Soviet engineers laid a further 6,000 mines which channelled the attacks by the German armour and brought about the destruction of at least 100 armoured vehicles. In the late afternoon troops of the German 86th Infantry Division had reached the outskirts of Ponyri. On the eastern flank of the main German thrust, 216th and 78th Infantry Divisions of General Freissner's XXIII Corps had launched a heavy attack against strongly defended road junction of Maloarkhangelsk. Here also, a detachment of Ferdinands were employed with their associated 'Goliath' demolition vehicles. Although the Germans succeeded in penetrating the outer defensive zone, the Russians' 129th Armoured Brigade launched a successful counter-attack. Nevertheless, by the

▲ *Many German vehicles like this assault gun ran on to mines and were destroyed, any surviving crews and supporting infantry being killed by Soviet gunners. Enmeshed in the defence lines, tanks fell prey to tank-hunters who emerged from their trenches to drop 'Molotov' Cocktails on the engine decks. (Novosti)*

end of the first day the divisions of XLVII and XLI Panzer Corps had pushed some four to six miles into the first Soviet defensive belt, but at great cost.

Although suspected, the strength and depth of the Soviet defences had come as a revelation to the Germans. Indeed, the main defence zone remained intact to a depth of between four and six miles and was, as evening fell, being rapidly reinforced. As the fighting continued, Rokossovsky deduced that Model would deploy the bulk of his armour in the Butyrki and Bobrik area where the heavy pounding of the Russian 15th Rifle Division offered an opening for the Germans to exploit. This would then place the main weight of their thrust line in the direction of Olkhovatka. Throughout the rest of the day a rapid re-deployment and reinforcement of Soviet units and reserves took place, in order to prepare for the great armoured confrontation expected on 6 July.

Fourth Panzer Army/Army Detachment 'Kempf'/ Voronezh Front

Vatutin had already decided that the German offensive was imminent, following the advance of the whole of Fourth Panzer Army on the afternoon of the previous day to a new position that allowed them to place artillery observers overlooking the Soviet defences. As on the Central Front, interrogation of prisoners in the early hours of the 5th had elicited sufficient information to persuade Vatutin to order 6th and 7th Guards Armies at 0230 to loose off their own 600-gun barrage, to disrupt the assembling German units. At 0330 hours the German artillery replied with a tremendous barrage along the entire front of Fourth Panzer Army. Official reports later stated that the Germans fired more shells in this barrage than they had throughout the entire Polish and French campaigns combined.

As the first reports came in from Chistyakov's 6th Guards, the numbers of Luftwaffe aircraft

1 *Throughout the night of 4/5 July, German engineers clear lanes in the known Soviet minefields.*

2 *At 0400 hrs the German barrage begins all along front of Fourth Panzer Army.*

SOV ⊠ 6 GUARDS

CHISTYAKOV

SOV ⊠ 67 GUARDS RIFLE

To Oboyan

Cherkasskoye

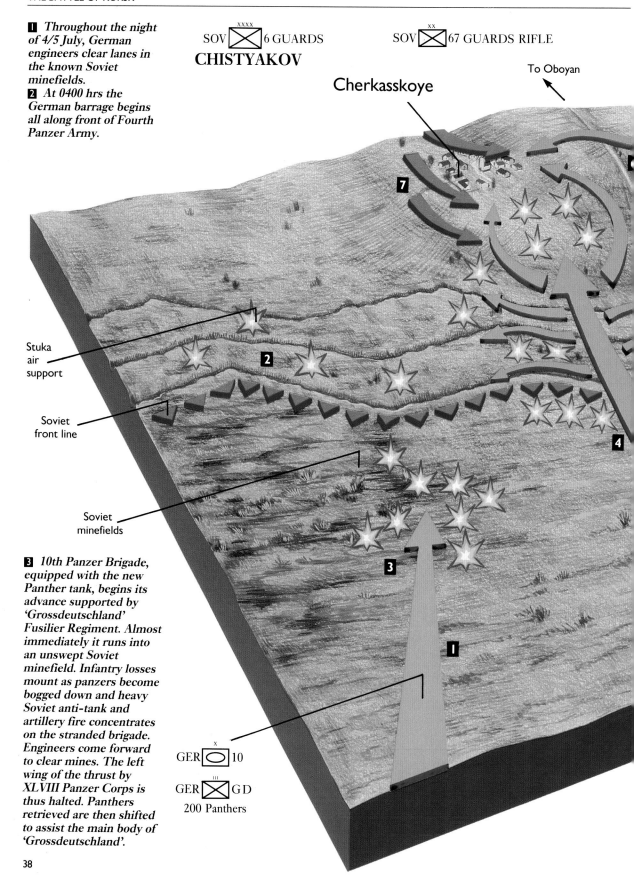

Stuka air support

Soviet front line

Soviet minefields

3 *10th Panzer Brigade, equipped with the new Panther tank, begins its advance supported by 'Grossdeutschland' Fusilier Regiment. Almost immediately it runs into an unswept Soviet minefield. Infantry losses mount as panzers become bogged down and heavy Soviet anti-tank and artillery fire concentrates on the stranded brigade. Engineers come forward to clear mines. The left wing of the thrust by XLVIII Panzer Corps is thus halted. Panthers retrieved are then shifted to assist the main body of 'Grossdeutschland'.*

GER ⬯ 10

GER ⊠ G D
200 Panthers

4 The assault by 'Grossdeutschland' main body goes in at 0500 hrs. At the point of the thrust the 'GD' Tiger company supported by Mark IVs, Mark IIIs, Panthers and assault guns effects a breach in the Soviet lines in front of Cherkasskoye. These lines are cleared in bitter fighting by the regimental Grenadier battalions; by 0915 the Germans are in front of the village.

5 To the right of 'Grossdeutschland' 11 Panzer division breaks through the Soviet defence lines.

6 Very heavy Soviet defence results in a litter of destroyed German tanks and smashed anti-tank guns in front of the village; an armoured combat group is detached from 11th Panzer Division to assault the eastern flank of the Soviet position.

7 Colonel-General Chistyakov, commander of Sixth Guards Army reinforces the 67th Guards Rifle Division with two regiments of anti-tank guns to block the German advance.

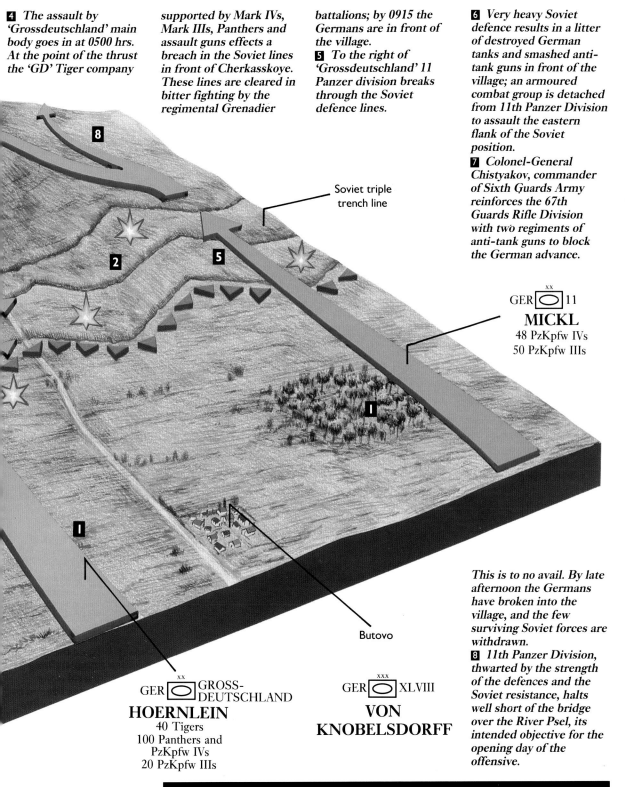

Soviet triple trench line

xx
GER ⬭ 11
MICKL
48 PzKpfw IVs
50 PzKpfw IIIs

Butovo

xx
GER ⬭ GROSS-DEUTSCHLAND
HOERNLEIN
40 Tigers
100 Panthers and PzKpfw IVs
20 PzKpfw IIIs

xxx
GER ⬭ XLVIII
VON KNOBELSDORFF

This is to no avail. By late afternoon the Germans have broken into the village, and the few surviving Soviet forces are withdrawn.

8 11th Panzer Division, thwarted by the strength of the defences and the Soviet resistance, halts well short of the bridge over the River Psel, its intended objective for the opening day of the offensive.

THE ASSAULT ON CHERKASSKOYE

by XLVIII Panzer Corps on 5 July 1943, as seen from the south

▲ *Throughout the first day of the offensive the Germans had air superiority over the* southern sector of the salient and their Stukas and other ground-support aircraft were able to attack *Soviet positions with impunity. This was vital for the Stukas whose targets were beyond the* point units of the advancing armour. Directed by Luftwaffe ground controllers, these dive-bombers were an important compensation for the Germans' weakness in artillery. (Bundesarchiv)

◄ *Two Ferdinands camouflaged against a tree line along the railway leading to the village of Ponyri. This small agricultural settlement was to become the focal point of savage fighting during the week-long offensive, being likened by German and Soviet alike to a mini 'Stalingrad'. (M. Jaugitz)*

supporting the advancing Fourth Panzer Army clearly indicated that a major plank in the Soviet plan had gone awry. An attempt by 2nd Air Army to destroy Luftwaffe aircraft on their airfields around Kharkov only moments before they were due to take off was forestalled when a Freya long-range radar station registered the massive incoming air strike. The Fw 190s and Bf 109s of JGs 3 and 52 were scrambled at the very last minute and managed to catch the Russian air armada short of the bases. In what was to be the largest air battle of the war, a huge mêlée involving more than 500 aircraft began. Russian losses, though not grievous, were sufficient to give the Luftwaffe air superiority over the battlefield during the first day of the offensive. More than 2,000 sorties were flown on the 5th in support of Fourth Panzer Army.

At 0400 Fourth Panzer Army went over to the offensive along the entire thirty miles of its front between Belgorod and Gertsovka. The panzers rumbled over the paths through the minefields that the sappers had spent most of the night clearing. In all, the 700 tanks and assault guns of two panzer corps smashed a huge mailed fist at Chistyakov's 6th Guards Army in the hope of destroying it and driving through the Soviet defences by the end of the day. Such expectations quickly broke down in the face of the sheer scale of the Soviet defences and as a consequence of other factors beyond the control of the planning staffs.

XLVIII Panzer Corps

The key to the success of General Otto von Knobelsdorff's XLVIII Panzer Corps, in breaking through the Soviet defences on each side of Butovo and executing a swift advance to the south bank of the Pena, was the massive concentration of power that lay with 10 Panzer Brigade, equipped with the new Panther. On paper these 200 machines gave the Panzer Corps an unprecedented concentration of armour and firepower. In the wake of the barrage, Panther Brigade 'Decker' moved off from Butovo, but almost immediately ran into a minefield that immobilized many of the vehicles. Others attempting to extricate themselves set off more mines. In front of Cherkasskoye, the initial objective of the offensive and a key position in the first Soviet defence line on this part of the front, more than 36 Panthers lay immobile. The Russians brought down intense artillery fire on the stationary tanks and on the engineers who went into the minefields to clear paths for those Panthers not too badly damaged and able to extricate themselves. In the meantime the infantry, who had been waiting for the Panther support, had attacked the Soviet positions, only to be thrown back with heavy casualties.

While the thrust of the Panther Brigade was stalled for several hours, 'Grossdeutschland' and 11th Panzer Division on the Corps' right wing, attacking towards Cherkasskoye in wedge formation, quickly broke into the Soviet first defence line and by 0915 were on the outskirts of the village. To hold this vital position the Russian 67th Guards Rifle Division was reinforced by two regiments of anti-tank guns and a vicious battle for control of the position raged throughout the day. By late afternoon the Russians had withdrawn, leaving the village in German hands.

On the extreme left of the Corps, 3rd Panzer Division had likewise fought against extremely strong Soviet resistance offered by 71st Guards Rifle Division. Supported by Stukas, the panzers and infantry of 332nd Division pushed slowly through the Soviet defence lines, encountering strong resistance all the way. By nightfall, however, 3rd Panzer Division had reached the River Pena, having penetrated some six miles into the Soviet lines. As dusk fell, the blue crayon on the situation map in Knobelsdorff's headquarters showed that his Panzer Corps had effected a substantial breach in the Soviet defences. Even so, compared to the timetable prepared by Hoth, the Corps was very short of its stated objectives. As elsewhere, the formidable nature of the defences and the tenacious and dogged resistance of the Soviet troops had taken a heavy toll of the German divisions.

While adhering to the OKH plan for 'Citadel', which required Fourth Panzer Army to link up with Ninth Army, Hoth had decided that before this could come about it would be necessary to deal with the Soviet reserves, amounting to several armoured corps, to the south-east of Kursk. Further to the north-east lay Rotmistrov's 5th

Von Manstein's Assault on the Voronezh Front, 5-14 July 1943

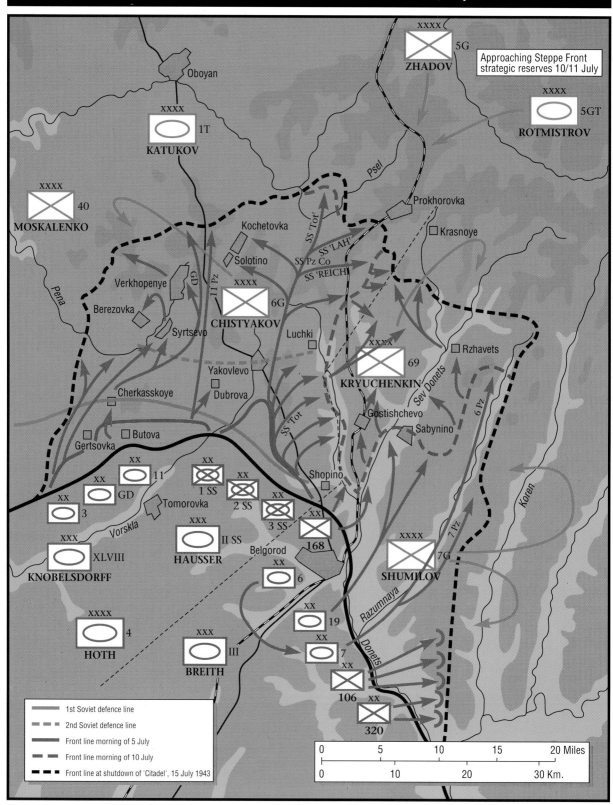

Approaching Steppe Front
strategic reserves 10/11 July

Legend:
- 1st Soviet defence line
- 2nd Soviet defence line
- Front line morning of 5 July
- Front line morning of 10 July
- Front line at shutdown of 'Citadel', 15 July 1943

| 0 | 5 | 10 | 15 | 20 Miles |

| 0 | 10 | 20 | 30 Km. |

◀ *Von Manstein's assault on the Voronezh Front, 5-14 July 1943. Of the two thrusts by Army Groups Centre and South on the Kursk salient, it was the latter that posed the greatest threat. Unlike Model, von Manstein grouped his Fourth Panzer Army's armour into a massive 'fist' of some 700 panzers. These were unleashed en masse on 5 July, but although their momentum took them deep into the Soviet defence lines, the sheer scale and depth of these and the tenacity of the Russian defenders exacted a very high price, both in tanks and dead and wounded men. By the end of the battle at Prokhorovka Soviet tank strength was down to 50 per cent of that available on 5 July, but when their counter-offensive began the Soviets had twice as many tanks as they had had when it started. German losses were irreplaceable. It was the way in which the Soviet defences had been designed expressly to 'bleed white' the German armour that has led to this episode being labelled 'the death ride of Fourth Panzer Army'.*

▶ *While 'Grossdeutschland' Division was crashing through the Soviet defence lines in front of the fortified village of Cherkasskoye, 'Combat Group Count Schimmelmann' of 11th Panzer Division attacked from the right flank with flame-throwing Panzer IIIs. The village, a major position in the first defence line, fell during the afternoon of 5 July. (Bundesarchiv)*

▲ *Panthers Ausf 'D' of 52nd Panzerabteilung, 10 Panzer Brigade at the halt. Caught by the camera prior to the start of their calamitous drive into the* minefields in front of the heavily fortified village of Cherkasskoye, the new Panthers of this brigade constituted the single most powerful armoured unit of all the German formations at Kursk, but their début was inauspicious to say the least. (Munin Verlag)

Guards Tank Army which formed part of the STAVKA reserve. It seemed highly likely that any blind adherence to the OKH plan would offer these forces a superb opportunity to attack the flank of Fourth Panzer Army as it swung towards Oboyan and joined battle with 1st Tank Army, which had been placed there by Vatutin specifically to block the advancing Germans. Assuming that this was indeed the Soviet intention, Hoth reckoned that the only direction from which the reserve armoured units and 5th Guards Tank Army could approach the flank of Fourth Panzer Army would be via the town of Prokhorovka. He therefore decided that as soon as the Soviet defence lines had been breached, he would turn all his offensive formations towards the north-east, and in so doing confound Soviet expectations and defeat the reserve armour in the vicinity of Prokhorovka. He would then wheel again towards Oboyan and from there drive through to Kursk to link up with Model's forces.

II SS Panzer Corps

It was this plan that accounted for the disposition of II SS Panzer Corps on 5 July. The three panzer grenadier divisions, 'Leibstandarte Adolf Hitler', 'Das Reich' and 'Totenkopf', were deployed in a parallel echelon to the right, ready for the push towards Prokhorovka. Although not designated full panzer divisions until after Kursk, they were formidably equipped with armour for the coming offensive, disposing of some 340 tanks and 195 self-propelled guns of all types. All three divisions deployed their own Tiger regiments. Conscious of the élite status of these units, the Soviets had emplaced before their line of advance very deeply echeloned fortifications occupied by the troops of the experienced 52nd Guards Rifle division and 375th Rifle division.

Moving forward at 0400, having traversed the minefields that had been cleared by the combat engineers, the three divisions deployed into the well-rehearsed *Panzerkeil*. At the point of the wedge were the Tigers, these being flanked by Panthers (in Das Reich) and the lighter, Mark III and IV medium tanks and assault guns, with the infantry following behind, either in tracked carriers or on foot. The divisions broke through the first line of defences comparatively quickly despite encountering large numbers of Soviet tanks, but, as elsewhere, once the initial gains had been made,

▼ *The Tigers of 3rd SS Panzer Grenadier Division 'Totenkopf' lead the advance into the Soviet first defence line on 5 July. With support from the divisional assault gun battalion a rapid breach of the Soviet line was* effected. *Although the infantry seem to be presenting a good target, they would dismount to clear out enemy positions using the Tigers and assault guns for cover. (Bundesarchiv)*

▲ Behind the point of the Panzerkeil formed by the divisional Tiger regiment, came the lighter Panzer Mark IIIs and IVs; the former are seen here. These are the late Panzerkampfwagen III Ausf 'L' and 'M', both mounting a long-barrelled 5.0cm KwK39 L/60 gun. The Battle of Kursk marked the swan-song of the Panzer III as a battletank. (Bundesarchiv)

▼ Well-camouflaged 7.62cm 'rauch-boom' anti-tank guns took a heavy toll of German armour. As part of the sophisticated defensive system the guns were deployed singly, or in 'Pakfronts' which presented a solid wall of fire from as many as twelve guns against German armour channelled across their field of fire by cunningly sited minefields. The German troops thought highly of this weapon and many captured in 1941 were re-chambered to take German ammunition and designated 7.62cm PaK 36/39(r). (Novosti)

Standard issue wear for Soviet tank crews at Kursk was the slate-grey or black coverall as seen in Figure 1. 2. The Red Army employed many women in combat roles such as this sniper in camouflage coverall and equipped with a Mosin 1891 rifle. The lieutenant of the Rifle Forces in Figure 3 illustrates the January 1943 uniform changes which saw the introduction of Tsarist-style rank insignia and new 'gymnastiorka' or blouse with stand-up collar and shoulder-boards.

▶ *In the wake of the panzers came the infantry, either on foot or perched on the supporting assault guns. In this photograph, again of 'Totenkopf' in action, an 8.0cm mortar team wanders past the camera while in the distance assault guns and other vehicles fan out as they cross the steppe. The nature of the terrain across which the SS Panzer Corps advanced in the scorching heat of the opening days of the offensive is evident; clearly there is little fear of minefields here. (Bundesarchiv)*

▶ *Against a backdrop of thick smoke, SS infantrymen make their way through a burning village. At least three Soviet prisoners are accompanying them as they advance. (Bundesarchiv)*

the formidable defences with innumerable anti-tank positions, minefields and ferocious artillery barrages slowed down the advance. By the end of the day, however, II SS Panzer Corps had broken through the anti-tank barriers and artillery positions of 52nd Guards Division and had penetrated some twenty kilometres into the defensive zone.

On the right wing of the Corps, in the fading light of the summer evening, assault units of SS 'Totenkopf' supported by Tigers seized an important 69th Army command post in the village of Yakhontovo. Apart from amply demonstrating the élan associated with the Waffen SS units, the comparatively rapid progress of the Corps through

the Soviet lines was brought about by a remarkable combination of concentrated firepower on the ground and very close air support. Without doubt the 41 Tigers available to the Corps on the 5th endowed the *Panzerkeil* of the SS Panzer Corps with great destructive power.

Overhead, relays of ground-attack aircraft blasted a corridor for the advancing SS divisions. In the forefront of the German air strikes was a number of Ju 87Gs equipped with 37mm twin cannon, under the command of the famous pilot Hans Rudel. Apart from the ubiquitous Stuka, Fw 190s dropped SD-1 and SD-2 high-fragmentation bombs on the Soviet defences along the line of march, wreaking havoc among the anti-tank gun

▲The advance of II SS Panzer Corps was greatly assisted by the the Schlachtflieger and the aircraft of the Panzerjäger-Staffeln. Junkers Ju 87G-1s armed with two 37mm cannon wrought havoc among the Soviet tanks along the line of advance. The technique had been developed by Karl Rudel, one of the Luftwaffe's top Stuka pilots. Approaching from the rear of the T-34, he would fire at the engine compartment which when hit exploded and destroyed the tank. This tactic was fine when the Germans had air superiority, but if Soviet fighters were present the Stuka was usually doomed. (Bundesarchiv)

▼Early on 6 July Rokossovsky ordered an armoured counter-attack against the German divisions that were bringing pressure to bear on 13th Army's front. 16th Tank Corps under the command of General Grigoyev launched their T-34s and T-70 light tanks against the German positions but were thrown back after engaging 2nd Panzer Division. (Novosti)

and artillery crews. In addition, Hs 129s armed with a belly-mounted 30mm cannon shot up Soviet armour and artillery positions. In this way the very heavily fortified Soviet villages of Berezov, Gremuchi, Bykovo, Kozma-Demyanovka and Voznesenski, all lying along the line of march of the SS Panzer corps, fell relatively quickly to the combined air and ground assault. The virtual air superiority enjoyed by the Luftwaffe over the southern part of the salient was a high price for the Soviets to pay for the failure of their pre-emptive strike on the German air bases earlier in the day. As dusk fell, the SS Panzer Corps was well placed to exploit its gains, but the Corps' losses had been heavy, the 'Leibstandarte' alone losing some 97 killed and 522 wounded. Along the entire length of Fourth Panzer Army's front the going had been very hard, but the Germans had managed to split 6th Guards Army's front in two places. It looked as though Hoth's plan, notwith-standing the slower than anticipated rate of advance, could still be carried out.

Army Detachment 'Kempf'

As the first day of 'Citadel' drew to a close, the only real cause for concern on the German side lay in the slow progress being made by the units of Army Detachment 'Kempf'. With three panzer divisions and 48 Tigers of schwere Panzer Abteilung 503, the Panzer Corps, its flank screened by the infantry divisions of the 'Raus' Special Attack Corps, was to penetrate the Soviet defences in the direction of Korocha as rapidly as possible. Here it would engage and defeat the Soviet armoured reserves that had been identified by aerial reconnaissance and which Hoth expected would strike at the right flank of the advancing SS Panzer Corps. Having achieved this objective, III Panzer Corps was to wheel to the north-west and be in position to assault the flank of Rotmistrov's 5th Guards Tank Army when it clashed with the Corps in the vicinity of Prokhorovka. Timing was therefore of the essence. If Kempf was to adhere to Hoth's timetable, an early breakthrough of the Soviet defence lines was vital. Here nature and the Soviets were to conspire to delay the Germans. In ferocious fighting, the troops of Shumilov's 7th Guards Army held the German armour and supporting infantry to positions very close to the Donets river crossings. To strengthen Shumilov and foil the German breakout, Vatutin dispatched three more rifle divisions to cover any possible German advance in the direction of Korocha.

As darkness fell, exhausted men on both sides caught what sleep they could. It was clear that by the end of the first day of Operation 'Citadel', the Germans had already made the essential moves that would govern the form and course of the remainder of the battle.

6–9 July: Ninth Army/Central Front

By the early hours of 6 July, Rokossovsky had completed the re-deployment of his forces in preparation for the resumption of the German offensive. The 18th Guards Rifle Division had been sent to strengthen the defence of Maloark-hangelsk, with 3rd Tank Corps stationed to the south of Ponyri. The 17th Guards Rifle Corps was moved to bolster 13th Army's defensive zone, and to cover the anticipated German thrust towards Olkhovatka he had stationed 19th Tank Corps to the west and 16th Tank Corps to the north-east of the town. The 16th Tank Corps launched an attack in the early morning of the 6th, with some 100 T-34s and T-70 light tanks. Having pene-trated some two miles, the Soviet force was thrown back by 2nd Panzer Division, which had just appeared on the battlefield. Deployed alongside the Panzer IVs and supporting assault guns were the Tigers of schwere Panzer Abteilung 505, now attached to 2nd Panzer Division. By mid-morning the sun was beating down from a cloudless sky on the patchwork of rye and wheat fields that dominated this sector of the front. Packets of German armour, painted sand-yellow broken up by shocks of red-brown and green, could be seen by the Soviets moving forward and manoeuvring into formation. Audible even above the cacophony of artillery fire now sweeping the battlefield was the distinctive howl of the German 'Nebelwerfer', whose launch was accompanied by a sea of flame and huge smoke plumes which inscribed great arcs across the sky before plunging into the Soviet lines. Salvo after salvo roared forth as the German

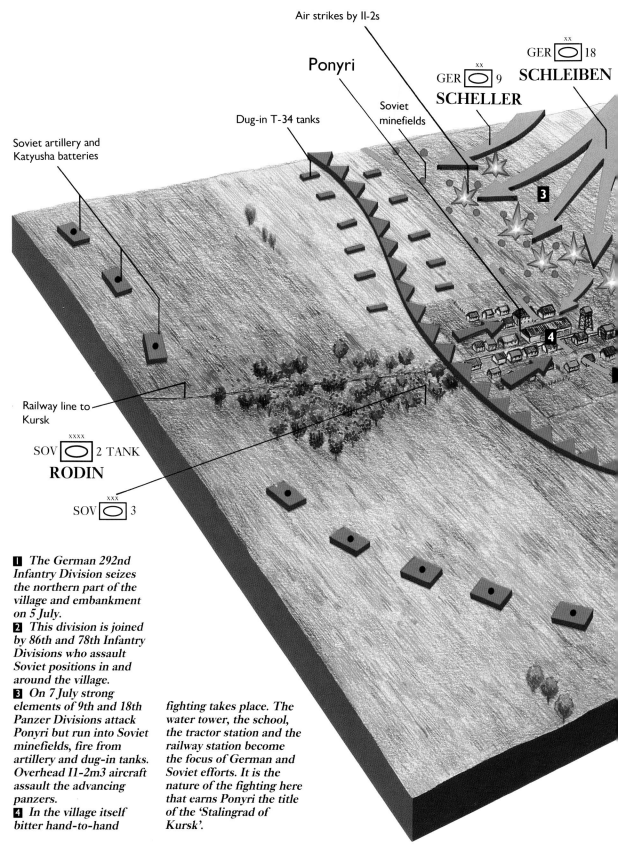

Air strikes by Il-2s

Ponyri

GER ⟨xx ◯⟩ 18 SCHLEIBEN

GER ⟨xx ◯⟩ 9 SCHELLER

Soviet minefields

Dug-in T-34 tanks

Soviet artillery and
Katyusha batteries

3

4

Railway line to
Kursk

SOV ⟨xxxx ◯⟩ 2 TANK
RODIN

SOV ⟨xxx ◯⟩ 3

1 The German 292nd
Infantry Division seizes
the northern part of the
village and embankment
on 5 July.

2 This division is joined
by 86th and 78th Infantry
Divisions who assault
Soviet positions in and
around the village.

3 On 7 July strong
elements of 9th and 18th
Panzer Divisions attack
Ponyri but run into Soviet
minefields, fire from
artillery and dug-in tanks.
Overhead I1-2m3 aircraft
assault the advancing
panzers.

4 In the village itself
bitter hand-to-hand

fighting takes place. The
water tower, the school,
the tractor station and the
railway station become
the focus of German and
Soviet efforts. It is the
nature of the fighting here
that earns Ponyri the title
of the 'Stalingrad of
Kursk'.

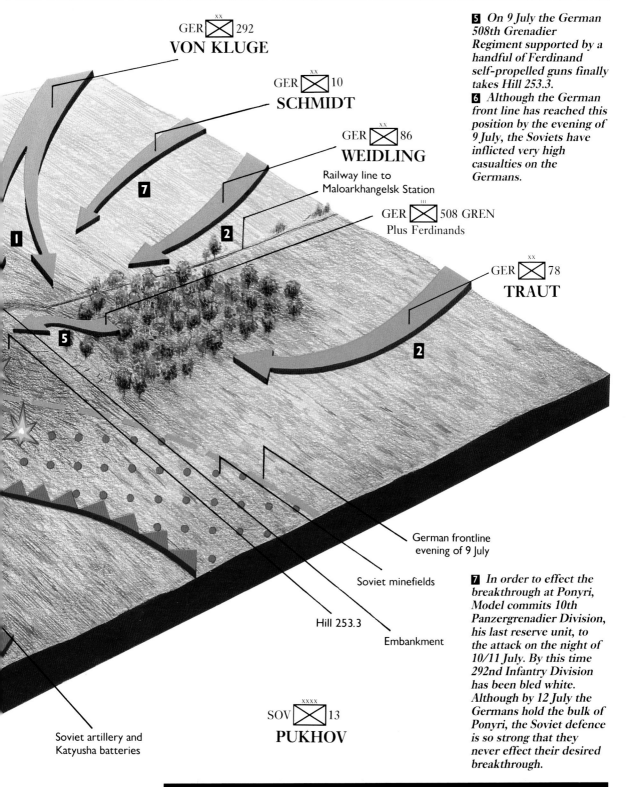

GER $\boxed{\times}^{xx}$ 292
VON KLUGE

GER $\boxed{\times}^{xx}$ 10
SCHMIDT

GER $\boxed{\times}^{xx}$ 86
WEIDLING

Railway line to
Maloarkhangelsk Station

GER $\boxed{\times}^{lll}$ 508 GREN
Plus Ferdinands

GER $\boxed{\times}^{xx}$ 78
TRAUT

5 *On 9 July the German 508th Grenadier Regiment supported by a handful of Ferdinand self-propelled guns finally takes Hill 253.3.*

6 *Although the German front line has reached this position by the evening of 9 July, the Soviets have inflicted very high casualties on the Germans.*

German frontline
evening of 9 July

Soviet minefields

Hill 253.3

Embankment

SOV $\boxed{\times}^{xxxx}$ 13
PUKHOV

Soviet artillery and
Katyusha batteries

7 *In order to effect the breakthrough at Ponyri, Model commits 10th Panzergrenadier Division, his last reserve unit, to the attack on the night of 10/11 July. By this time 292nd Infantry Division has been bled white. Although by 12 July the Germans hold the bulk of Ponyri, the Soviet defence is so strong that they never effect their desired breakthrough.*

THE BATTLE FOR PONYRI

5–12 July 1943, as seen from the south-east

barrage swept the defences ahead of the advancing panzers. In reply, the Soviets unleashed their massed Katyusha batteries to augment the gun barrage which now descended on the infantry following the advancing panzer wedges.

From the German positions it could be seen through the heat haze that the horizon was dominated by a low ridge, centred on Hill 274 and the village of Olkhovatka. Model was convinced that its possession was the key that would unlock the Soviet defences and open the way for Ninth Army to drive on Kursk. Rokossovsky, equally aware of the significance of the position, had disposed his forces, particularly his armour, to take account of German intentions, and to block any attempt to reach and take the town. In fact, even before 'Citadel' was launched, the strategic significance of Olkhovatka had been appreciated, and the ground between Soborovka and the hills, that is, on a heading approximating to Model's main thrust line, had been repeatedly turned over by the civilians and troops preparing the defences. The Germans were, in effect, about to launch their attack against one of the strongest and most sophisticated sections of the main defensive belt.

As the German advance began, the panzers deployed in their characteristic wedge in formations of a hundred tanks or more. The Tigers, exploiting their heavy armour and firepower, thrust

▲ *Panzer IIIs and IVs of 2nd Panzer Division deploying for the attempt to force the Soviet defences in the direction of Olkhovatka. While this attack had the Tigers of* *schwere Panzerabteilung 505 at the point, the great majority of tanks on Ninth Army's front were Mark IIIs and IVs. (Bundesarchiv)*

ahead and seized the village of Soborovka. The Germans now began to feed more and more armour on to the battlefield, with 9th Panzer Division deploying alongside the other panzer divisions between the villages of Soborovka and Pervyye Ponyri. By midday the Germans had no fewer than 1,000 tanks in action along the 6-mile front between the two villages and were supported by more than 3,000 guns and mortars. Against this massive force the Soviets deployed as many tanks and assault guns of their own. The Germans attempted to advance against this mass of Soviet armour, composed almost entirely of T-34s, while at the same time contending with the extremely complex and extensive defences. The point of the German assault was provided by the remaining Tigers of Abteilung 505, but even their thick armour and powerful 8.8cm guns proved of little avail.

The carefully prepared anti-tank 'resistance points' now came into their own. Penned in the defence zones, the Tigers and Panzer IVs were

▲ ▶ *A 30cm Nebelwerfer prepares to launch in support of Model's attack on 6 July. With these weapons the Germans, like the Russians with their 'Katyusha' launchers, could deliver a heavy and concentrated barrage. Not the least frightful aspect of the German weapon was the noise it made as it 'rocketed' through the air. Its relative light weight and mobility compared to conventional artillery made it a very effective weapon. (Bundesarchiv)*

dispatched by dug-in T-34s, ' Pakfronts' or the numerous anti-tank rifles firing from superbly camouflaged positions. Others fell prey to mines or to infantrymen who, having let the tanks pass, rose from their trenches and lobbed their 'Molotov' cocktails on to the engine decks of the panzers and assault guns. German infantry following behind the tanks were cut down by machine-gun or mortars. Entire infantry units melted away in the fiery furnace. Shturmoviks and Stukas attacked ground targets ceaselessly. Time and again the tanks of 2nd and 9th Panzer attacked, were repulsed, regrouped and were thrown forward again, only to be repulsed yet again. By evening, when the fighting had abated, the offensive power of the two Tiger regiments had been shattered. Numerous Tigers and other tanks lay destroyed or abandoned in the Soviet lines, mute testimony to the effectiveness of the defence system and the tenacity of the defenders. This German failure was compounded by the repulse of a further attempt by XXIII Corps to storm Maloarkhangelsk. As darkness fell many panzer crews, who had not slept for two days, dropped from their machines to snatch what sleep they could, oblivious of the star-shells that lit up the darkness, and the staccato rattle of machine-guns, signifying the savage fire fights that continued throughout the night as the

▲'The Tigers are burning!'. The Soviets considered the destruction of large numbers of Tigers as a telling indication that the Germans had lost the battle. By nightfall on 6 July the two battalions of schwere Panzerabteilung 505 had been shattered by the power of the Soviet defences and many panzers lay destroyed or abandoned in the defence lines. (Bundsarchiv)

German infantry clashed with Soviet tank-hunting teams amidst the trench systems.

On 7 and 8 July Model tried again, but this time committing his forces on a wider front than on the previous day. In the wake of the German assault on the 6th, Rokossovsky, to strengthen his reserves, had pulled in units from the relatively quiescent sectors of the line covered by 60th and 65th Armies. The former had to surrender a division that was rapidly shifted, lock, stock and barrel, to support 13th Army, and 65th Army lost two tank regiments.

All Soviet armour in the line was ordered to dig in and leave only their turrets showing. Soviet tank losses had been high, particularly to the Tigers, whose 8.8cm gun easily out-ranged the 7.62cm main gun of the T-34, when engaged in the longer-range fire fights. As the German attacks unfolded on the 7th, the Soviets proceeded from the assumption that the Olkhovatka sector was still the main axis. This analysis in no way ignored the ferocity of the fighting elsewhere, as for example the days-long contest for the agricultural village of Ponyri and Hill 253.5. The fighting for this small settlement was likened by Germans and Russians alike to a miniature 'Stalingrad'. Lying along the railway running from Orel to Kursk, its local importance was as a collection and distribution point for produce and machinery for the collective farms in the vicinity. For six days this ramshackle village became the focal point of immense efforts by both sides. The Germans hoped that by committing strong armoured forces the settlement could be taken, which would allow the panzers to break into the open country beyond the village, and then roll up the Soviet defence lines. The Soviets

▶ *An integral part of the Soviet plan for the conduct of the battle required a mass attack by partisans against the German lines of communication leading to the front. A sustained campaign of attacks on the railways and road transport not only destroyed a great deal of matériel, but also tied down large numbers of German troops in anti-partisan sweeps. Here a mass swearing-in of new Party members is taking place, an event not uncommon at this time when Party membership in the army and among the partisans rose dramatically. (Novosti)*

KV-1 Model 1941. Only some 205 of the Soviet tanks used at Kursk were classed as heavies, Kursk marking the swansong of the KV-1. Many were destroyed at long range by the guns of the Tigers and Panthers. This example bears the turret slogan 'Twenty-Fifth of October'.

◀ *Ilyushin Il-2m3s armed with 37mm cannon emulated their German counterparts by attacking tanks – and with as much success. On 7 July the panzers of 9th Panzer Division were subjected to prolonged strafing as they fought their way through the defences before Ponyri. The Soviets claimed that the Shturmoviki destroyed at least 60 panzers in the attack. (Novosti)*

◀▶ *By 9 July the struggle to win the village of Ponyri had witnessed some of the most savage fighting of the entire battle. On that date six 'Ferdinands' were deployed to assault Hill 253.3 It was hoped that their heavy armour would take them through the Soviet defences unscathed and enable their accompanying infantry to roll up the Soviet positions. The defences proved too tough, however, even for the Ferdinands. In the second of this sequence of photographs a Ferdinand has just detonated a mine and has started to burn. (M. Jaugitz)*

were determined to prevent this and fed in strong reserves to bolster their position.

Units of 292nd Infantry division had captured the railway embankment and the northern part of the village on the opening day of the offensive, but by the 6th the struggle for control of the settlement was sucking in large numbers of German units. To support 292nd Infantry Division's endeavour to storm the remainder of the village, Model fed in 9th and 18th Panzer Divisions and 86th Infantry

Division. The Soviets reciprocated in kind, feeding in more artillery, mortars and howitzers. As in the approaches to Olkhovatka, many of the tanks were dug in to bolster the already formidable defences around the settlement. On the 7th a German attack by some 300 panzers clashed head-on with the T-34s of 16th and 19th Tank Corps. In Ponyri itself, ferocious hand-to-hand fighting took place with heavy fire support from tanks, artillery and SP guns, as both sides contested the salient features. From 6 to 9 July a see-saw struggle for control of the schoolhouse, tractor depot, railway station and water tower, took place. As elsewhere, German massed tank attacks impaled themselves upon the minefields and were shattered by the massed fire from T-34s, anti-tank guns and tank-hunting units with their anti-tank rifles and 'Molotov' cocktails. On the 9th the Germans attacked again, using half-a-dozen Ferdinand SP guns as fire support, in a bid to take Hill 253.5, to the immediate north-east of the village.

The Russians were certainly right in their perception that Olkhovatka was still Model's principal target. Notwithstanding the losses of the 6th, he proceeded to reorganize his units and on the 7th was again ready to send in his panzers and infantry to effect the breakthrough. The determination to achieve this objective, can be measured by the very rapid re-deployment of nearly 50

▼*A German 10.5cm leFH18/3 fires; the ammunition number stands ready to push a new shell into the breach. The volume of artillery fire from German and Soviet guns which preceded and continued during the course of Model's attack on 7 July temporarily 'darkened the sun' as vast quantities of smoke filled the air. Complementing this continual barrage were the bombings from Luftwaffe and Soviet Air Force aircraft. (Bundesarchiv)*

per cent of Luftflotte 4's aircraft from the southern part of the salient, to support Ninth Army's drive. By 0900 the Soviets could see the masses of German armour and their attendant armoured personnel carriers, deploying for the attack. Model's assumption was that the sheer weight of the German armoured fist must in the end break through, and in the fallacy of that assumption lay the key to the Red Army's victory on this battlefield. Although the Soviets were experiencing frightful losses from a concentration of firepower never before experienced, the defences were fulfilling the purpose for which they were designed. Each German attack was sucking in more and more armour, to replace the shattered and blackened hulks that now littered and marked the German advance. Despite the damage the Germans were inflicting on the defenders, the central task of 'bleeding white' the German armour was being realized.

As the artillery and Luftwaffe bombarded the defences, the attack resolved itself into two thrusts: 2nd and 20th Panzer Divisions heading for Samodurovka–Teploye–Molotychi and, farther to the east, 18th and 19th Panzer Divisions bringing pressure to bear on Olkhovatka once again. Although Rokossovsky had reinforced these positions, the addition of von Saucken's 4th Panzer Division to the thrust towards Samodurovka saw the Soviet line finally crack along that axis, when

▲Panzer Mark IIIs of General von Saucken's 4th Panzer Division prepare for the attack on Samodurovka in a bid to smash the defences and enable the breakthrough to Kursk to begin. The presence of vegetation for camouflage on the tanks suggests that the Soviet Air Force has been quite diligent in its attention to German armour moving towards the front line. (Bundesarchiv)

some 300 panzers, massed on a very narrow frontage, finally crashed through the Soviet positions. The following day the Germans maintained the pressure, deploying four panzer divisions supported by 6th Infantry Division along the entire length of a 10-mile line stretching from Samodurovka to Pervyye Ponyri. Fourth Panzer Division was now launched alongside 2nd and 20th Panzer Divisions against the Soviet defences around Teploye. During the next three days a see-saw battle for control of the village raged, both sides feeding in large numbers of tanks and infantry with powerful air support and artillery. Even the Tigers of Abteilung 505's third regiment were unable to penetrate the defences. Although the Germans finally took the village, the three attempts to storm the heights beyond were thrown back by ferocious resistance. Panzer attacks wilted in the hurricane of artillery fire called down upon them. A few miles to the east, in front of Olkhovatka, repeated attacks against the Soviet lines finally broke the anti-tank defences, allowing the

Apparent from the extensive Waffen SS photo archive covering 'Citadel' is the wide variation in uniforms worn by the troops in the battle. Figure 2 depicts an SS-schutze; figure 3 an infantry Unterscharführer. Both are fairly typical of the appearance of the bulk of the Waffen SS at Kursk.

Figure 1 depicts a Reiter of the SS-Kavallerie Division, which was not present at Kursk; he wears a smock and Bergmütze worn by many troops employed in the battle.

German forces to push forward to the slopes of the escarpment. Repeated attacks against the defences dug into the slopes, and sited on top of Hill 274, once more proved a drain on the German assault forces. Amid a desolation of gutted German and Soviet tanks, shattered anti-tank positions and the dead of both sides, 6th Infantry Division attacked the slopes of Hill 274 on the afternoon of 9 July. In a ferocious assault, the German infantry threw themselves against the Soviet trench lines cut into the lower slopes of the escarpment, but were brought to a halt in the welter of trenches, barbed wire and mines, and forced to withdraw under incessant artillery fire and local counter-attacks by Soviet infantry. As at Teploye, this surge marked the high tide of the German advance in the northern sector of the salient. Although the next few days would see renewed attempts to break through, the wrack of shattered panzers marking Ninth Army's advance bore mute testament to the fact that the momentum of Model's offensive was already beginning to decay.

6-9 July: II SS Panzer Corps and XLVIII Panzer Corps

In the evening of 5 July, Vatutin realized that the Germans had made larger inroads than had been expected. The greatest threat was emerging in the sector of II SS Panzer Corps which by nightfall had penetrated the first line of defences and stood poised to tackle the second line at dawn. While the progress made by XLVIII Panzer Corps had been less serious, their conjunction with the SS Panzer Corps was perceived by Vatutin as posing a grave threat to the integrity of 6th Guards Army's front, and the need to bring up reserves to cover the approaches to Oboyan was now seen to be very necessary. Indeed, the situation was considered so serious that Stalin had to tell Rokossovsky that he was diverting 27th Army, earlier promised to the Central Front, southwards to reinforce those other units that Vatutin was re-deploying to cover the Oboyan axis. Katukov's 1st Tank Army, with its 640 tanks, was therefore ordered south together with 2nd and 5th Guards Tank Corps into the rear of Chistyakov's 6th Guards Army. When Vatutin proposed using the T-34s and the few KV-1s of

Katukov's Tank Army to counter-attack Fourth Panzer Army the following morning, a heated debate ensued, Katukov pointing out that too many Soviet tanks were already being destroyed at long range by the guns of the Tigers and Panthers. It was therefore decided that the tanks would be dug in, as had been done on the Central Front, with only their turrets showing, to block any German advance on Oboyan.

In the early hours of the 6th the Panzers of the SS Panzer Corps took on ammunition and fuel and prepared to resume the offensive. 'Leibstandarte' and 'Das Reich' thrust northward, the Tigers of both divisions at the point, a total of 120 tanks advancing along the Belgorod–Oboyan road. In the vicinity of Yakovlevo, 'Leibstandarte' clashed with the tanks of 1st Armoured Guards Brigade and a fierce battle developed. 'On separate slopes, some 1,000 metres apart, the forces faced one another like figures on a chess-board, trying to influence fate, move by move, in their own favour. All the Tigers fired. The combat escalated into an ecstasy of roaring engines. The humans who directed and serviced them had to be calm; very calm, they aimed rapidly, they loaded rapidly, they gave orders quickly. They rolled ahead a few metres, pulled left, pulled right, manoeuvred to escape the enemy crosshairs and bring the enemy into their own fire. We counted the torches of enemy tanks which would never again fire on German soldiers. After one hour, twelve T-34s were in flames. The other thirty curved wildly back and forth, firing as rapidly as their barrels would deliver. they aimed well, but our armour was very strong. We no longer twitched when a steely finger knocked on our walls. We wiped the flakes of interior paint from our faces, loaded again, aimed, fired.'

With close air support the German armour crashed through the Soviet defences and by 1100 had overrun 155th Guards Rifle Regiment and breached the defensive barrier covering the Belgorod–Kursk highway. At midday 'Der Führer' Regiment of SS 'Reich' seized the village of Luchki. The consequence of this audacious *coup de main* was the opening of a huge gap in the defences of Chistyakov's Sixth Guards Army through which Hausser promptly pushed his

►*As the Tigers of 'Leibstandarte' and 'Das Reich' thrust northward in the direction of Oboyan, a tank battle of some size broke out in the vicinity of Yakovlevo. With visibility maximized by the steppe terrain, the gunners were able to use the long range of their 8.8cm KwK 36(L/56) gun to the full. Opening up at ranges far in excess of those of the T-34's 7.62cm gun, the Tigers destroyed many of them before the Soviets quit the field. Whereas the 7.62cm BP-350P HVAP9 (High-Velocity Armour-Piercing) shell of the T-34 could penetrate 94mm of armour at 500 metres, the Tiger's 8.8cm could penetrate the 47mm frontal armour of the Soviet tank out to a range of at least 1,500 metres. This clearly put the Soviet tank at a major disadvantage in tank duels and perhaps explains the decision by Rokossovsky and Vatutin to dig in their T-34s on certain sectors of their fronts. (Bundsarchiv)*

►*Panthers of 'Das Reich' take on ammunition in the early morning of 6 July before pushing on with the Tigers into the second major Soviet defence line. The Panther Ausf 'D', like the slightly later 'A', could carry 79 rounds of varying types of ammunition. Using the armour-piercing PzGr 40 round, the Panther could penetrate any known tank at the time. The frontal armour of the T-34 could be penetrated out to 800 metres whereas the thinner side and rear armour of the same tank could be penetrated at 2,800 metres. (Bundesarchiv).*

◀ The advance of the panzer divisions on 7 July was supported by 'Wespe' batteries of the mobile divisional artillery. A self-propelled tracked carriage mounting the 10.5cm leFH18M L/28 light howitzer, the Wespe proved itself first at Kursk and afterwards to be a very effective vehicle. Approximately 682 'Wespe' were produced from 1942 until 1944. (Bundesarchiv).

◀ Until 8 July the bulk of 'Totenkopf' found itself being employed as a flank guard for the other two SS divisions as they advanced north, a situation brought about by the failure of Army Detachment 'Kempf' to keep up with the advance as originally planned. The assault gun battalion of the division was in action extensively as 69th Army units with tank support attempted to drive into the rear of the SS Panzer Corps. 'Totenkopf' was finally relieved by 167th Infantry Division in the evening of 8 July whereupon it moved north to join up with the rest of the corps, prior to the move north-eastwards towards Prokhorovka on the 9th. (Bundesarchiv)

◀ Kursk marked the last time that Soviet prisoners in any numbers were captured by the Germans. According to German sources, by the time Hitler called off 'Citadel' on 13 July more than 34,000 Soviet soldiers were captives of Army Group South. In accordance with the original rationale laid down for the offensive in April, many of those shown in this picture were taken to Germany as slave labour. (Bundesarchiv)

Tiger E. 3rd SS Panzer Grenadier Division 'Totenkopf' deployed a company of fifteen Tiger 1s during 'Citadel'. The company commander's Tiger was designated '100' with the other Tigers carrying the standard three-digit code. 'Totenkopf' panzers carried the special Kursk marking illustrated; this was also employed by the 6th Panzer Division during the offensive.

panzers and motorized infantry. By the end of 6 July SS Panzer Corps was firmly ensconced in the Soviet second defence line. However, the failure of 'Kempf's forces on the right wing of II SS Panzer Corps to advance in parallel, as had been planned, had exposed the flank of the Corps as it moved north, and Hausser had to leave behind mobile units, as substitutes for his lack of infantry units, to counter the very frequent Soviet infantry attacks. Indeed, the shortage of infantry units now began to make itself generally felt; by the evening of the 6th more than 30 per cent of von Manstein's total armour was being used to defend the flanks. As late as 8 July 'Totenkopf' found itself acting as flank guard for the remainder of the Corps, and tied down by infantry attacks which by now had been reinforced with armour.

In response to the German advance STAVKA dispatched 2nd and 10th Tank Corps to the Prokhorovka area and at 2300 issued orders for the re-deployment of 5th Guards Tank Army from its leaguer positions as part of the reserve Steppe Front. For Rotmistrov, the order entailed force-marching all his armour and supporting units 190 miles so as to re-assemble for action in the vicinity of Prokhorovka by 9 July. Although the Germans appeared to be making substantial inroads into the Soviet defences, there could be no doubting that

it was at substantial cost. The 'Leibstandarte' war diary for the 6th admitted to 84 dead and 384 wounded. On the evening of the 6th Vatutin told Stalin by telephone that some 332 German tanks had been destroyed on Chistyakov's sector where 6th Guards, although being pushed back, had fought off twelve German attacks in the course of the day; Shumilov's 7th Guards having killed at least 10,000 of the enemy. As on the Central Front, the Germans were inflicting heavy casualties on the Red Army units, but these could be absorbed in the longer term; more importantly, the defensive strategy was succeeding in its primary task – the attrition of German armour. Stalin reiterated that the primary task of Vatutin's forces was to continue to wear the Germans down; the situation was not yet ripe for the planned counteroffensive.

The 7th of July was a day of major developments along the whole of Fourth Panzer Army's front. In the mist-shrouded dawn 'Leibstandarte' and 'Reich' Divisions resumed their driving attack north-west towards Oboyan. On XLVIII Panzer Corps' front, a major thrust by massed German armour began shortly after 0400 when some 400 tanks of 3rd and 11th Panzer Divisions, in conjunction with 'Grossdeutschland', attacked 3rd Mechanized and 31st Armoured Corps of Katukov's 1st Guards Tank Army. The previous day and much of the night of the 6th had seen all the Corps' units engaged in ferocious fighting as they assaulted the dug-in T-34s, anti-tank guns and flame-throwers that constituted the formidable second line of defence. With panzers and assault guns in support, the infantry cleared paths through the minefields and fought their way hand-to-hand into the enemy's positions. The contestants grappled with one another across ground transformed into a morass by intermittent thunderstorms which flooded the numerous small streams bisecting the terrain.

At first light on the 7th the German armour of XLVIII Panzer Corps supported by heavy artillery resumed its advance, attacking the Soviet positions between Syrtsevo and Yakovlevo. Dubrova was rapidly taken. Heavy German pressure now ruptured the front of the remaining units of 6th Guards Army which began a disorderly retreat. As the day advanced, however, the Soviets called in air support and the advancing German armour was dive-bombed heavily. Soviet tanks also appeared in greater numbers, taking advantage of the loss of German air superiority. Nevertheless, the German pressure began to build and the Soviet forces were pushed back to Syrtsevo, the last strongpoint guarding the defence line before Oboyan. 11th Panzer Division had already thrust to the north of the village and now lay astride the Belgorod-Kursk road to the east. In the teeth of extremely stubborn resistance 'Grossdeutschland' managed to storm the hills on each side of Syrtsevo, but an attempt to seize the village by frontal assault ground to a halt as the panzers, including Panthers, blundered into minefields and were shot up by the strong anti-tank gun defences. Even so, the Soviet position was becoming precarious, Major General Popiel later observing that in his view 7 July was one of the hardest days in the Battle of Kursk.

The achievement of XLVIII Panzer Corps on the 7th July was compounded by the success of II SS Panzer Corps. The latter's initial objective was the village of Teterevino, where aerial reconnaissance had reported the presence of Soviet armour in strength. Preceded by ground-attack aircraft (Meyer's Henschels and Druschel's Focke-Wulfs), the SS armour thrust towards Teterevino.

Breaking through the outer defences, the panzers encountered the main defence lines before the settlement. A savage fire fight began between the armour and the emplaced anti-tank guns, artillery and T-34s; the struggle against 29th Anti-tank Brigade lasted all afternoon. Through the gaps torn open by the Tigers an assault group stormed the village, capturing the command post and the entire staff of a rifle brigade. The fall of Teterevino and the subsequent drive by elements of 'Leibstandarte' and 'Totenkopf' towards Greznoye enabled the Waffen SS to break into the last Soviet defence lines in front of the River Psel. Other SS units wheeled north-east, and struck out towards Prokhorovka. In the wake of the advancing units came the SS Feldpolizei, rounding up listless prisoners and herding them to the rear in a scene reminiscent of the previous years of the Russian campaign, when such signs presaged an imminent Soviet collapse. 6th Guards Army's front was now in tatters, and there was a very real prospect that the Germans would, after all, succeed in reaching Oboyan.

Soviet positions throughout the whole of the south of the salient were now under threat. In the face of this dire situation Vatutin and Khrushchev issued the categorical order: 'On no account must the Germans break through to Oboyan.' Continual German pressure against the entire extent of 6th Guards' front saw even those Soviet units dispatched to plug the gaps melt away in the ferocity of the fighting. During a meeting later that evening at First Tank Army Headquarters, it became clear that the Soviets had found the heavy armour and firepower of the panzers, particularly the Tiger, operating in concert with the almost continual air support of the Schlachtgruppen, a potent and difficult combination to defeat. Nevertheless, Khrushchev, speaking with his full authority as Military Council Member, addressed the assembled commanders in unequivocal terms: 'The next two or three days will be terrible. Either we hold out or the Germans take Kursk. They are staking everything on this one card. For them it is a matter of life or death. We must see to it that they break their necks!' A rash of orders now emanated from Vatutin. Most of the armour and artillery of Moskalenko's 40th Army was fed into

▶ *A 'Das Reich' Panther commander signals to the others alongside to maintain formation as they move across the open steppe. It was under these circumstances that the Panther, as with the Tiger, could extract maximum benefit from the range advantage of its 7.5cm gun. (Bundesarchiv)*

▼ *Mute and inglorious! Two burnt-out victims have fallen to the guns of the SS Panzer Corps' Tigers. On the right is an SU-122 which was designed essentially for direct fire support of infantry or tank formations. However, its performance in the anti-* *tank role was poor, its HEAT (High-Explosive Anti-Tank) round proving a disappointment. The Soviet Samokhodnaya Ustanovka or SU series of* *armoured, turretless self-propelled guns were modelled on the successful German Sturmgeschützen (assault guns), first encountered in* *1941. On the left is a T-34 Model 1943, probably produced at Zavod nr.183, the Ural tank works at Nizhni Tagil. (Bundesarchiv)*

the line to support 1st Tank and 6th Guards Armies. Two counter-attacks were ordered for the 8th, to be directed against Fourth Panzer Army to relieve pressure on the units covering the approaches to Oboyan. All through the night the orders flowed and the divisions and armour redeployed in preparation for the next day's operations.

At dawn on 8 July the Germans resumed their push with 'Grossdeutschland' thrusting to take Syrtsevo. An attack by Soviet 40th Army was weathered. In the late morning some forty T-34s of General Krivoshein's III Mechanized Corps sortied from Syrtsevo in a desperate bid to stop the German advance, but ran across the guns of the Tiger company of 'Grossdeutschland'. In the

battle that followed ten T-34s were destroyed and the survivors rapidly vacated the battlefield as the German armour moved forward. Around the fortified town the defenders began to waver, at which units of 'Grossdeutschland' and 3rd Panzer Division drove forward to take advantage of the growing confusion and panic. Shortly after noon the town fell and the Soviet forces pulled back across the River Pena. A rapid follow-up by the divisional reconnaissance battalion, supported by an assault gun battalion, pushed forward to the town of Verkhopenye. The significance of this town lay in its bridge across the Pena which the Soviets were determined to hold. A major tank sortie of at least forty T-34s and M-3s was launched against the German units. The battle

▲ On the afternoon of 8 July 3rd Panzer Division deployed to advance on Syrtsevo, a fortified town in the Soviet second defence zone. Here a line of Panzer IIIs advance in the direction of the hilltop settlement. To the right can be seen the wreckage of a burning Soviet aircraft. Strength returns for 3rd Panzer Division prior to the start of 'Citadel' indicate that it was fielding 33 Panzer IVs and 30 Panzer IIIs. (Bundesarchiv)

▼ The Henschel Hs 129s, called up by Hauptmann Bruno Meyer to deal with the unexpected Soviet armoured incursion against the southern flank of the SS Panzer Corps on 8 July, were 'scrambled' from their base at Mikoyanovka, a large Luftwaffe airfield near Kharkov. The Hs 129s shared the base with Kampfgruppen He 111s and Ju-88s. Mikoyanovka had been one of the bases targeted by the Soviet Air Force in its abortive pre-emptive strike on the opening day of the German offensive. (Bundesarchiv)

raged for three hours, the German assault guns accounting for 35 Soviet tanks by late afternoon.

To the south, history of a different sort was being made. Very late in the evening of 7 July, the commander of Soviet 2nd Guards Tank Corps was ordered to assemble an armoured force with infantry support and strike westwards, from its position in the woods, around the village of Gostishchevo. Its task was to assault the deep flank of the SS Panzer Corps, with a view to cutting off its supply route. Quite by chance, as this completely unsuspected Soviet unit was emerging from woodland and deploying for attack with infantry in support, it was spotted by Hauptmann Meyer who was leading a flight of Henschel Hs 129s in a routine reconnaissance of the area. The Henschels devastated the T-34s with their 30mm cannon. Fw 190s of Battle Formation 'Druschel' flew in support, dropping anti-personnel bombs on the infantry. Within an hour fifty shattered T-34s

Henschel Hs-129B of 8 Staffel/Schlacht-geschwader (Sch.G) 1 armed with underfuselage-mounted 30mm Mk 101 cannon. Of particular note was the mass employment of this type in the destruction of a Soviet tank attack on the flank of the SS Panzer Corps on 8 July.

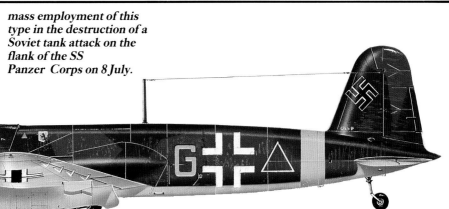

Fw 190 A-4s of Gefechtsverband (Battle Formation) Druschel (11/Sch.G.1) operated closely with the Hs 129s throughout 'Citadel' using SD-1 and SD-2 fragmentation bombs. Their employment in support of the SS Panzer Corps played a significant part in its early advance through the Soviet defences.

The Yakovlev Yak 1M entered service in 1942 and alongside the Yak 3, employed for the first time at Kursk, the Soviet Air Force began deploying fighter aircraft that were technically as good as those of the Luftwaffe. Over the battlefield of Kursk the Soviets for the first time wrested control of the air from the Germans.

The foremost Soviet ground attack type at Kursk (as indeed it was throughout the war) was the Ilyushin Il-2 'Shturmovik'. The Il-2m3 shown here introduced a rear gunner and heavier armour. Il-2s equipped with 37mm underwing cannon destroyed many tanks of the 9th Panzer Division on the Central Front.

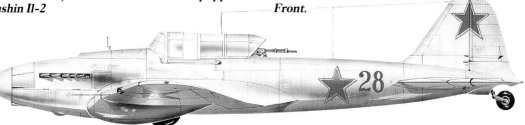

◄▼ *On 8 July an assault gun battalion supporting a reconnaissance unit advancing on the town of Verkopenye fought a battle against Soviet tanks, thirty-five of which were destroyed including a number of Lend Lease M3 Lees. In total the United States supplied the Soviet Union with 1,386 M3s. This tank was not at all popular with Soviet tankers who called it 'a grave for seven brothers' because of its vulnerability to German fire and its tendency to burn easily once hit. (Bundesarchiv)*

littered the battlefield. It was the first time in the history of warfare that a tank formation had been destroyed solely from the air.

Throughout this day and the 9th, Fourth Panzer Army launched successive attacks against the approaches to Oboyan. Mighty armoured fists pounded and battered 1st Tank and 6th Guards Armies which, by the afternoon of the 8th, were receiving reinforcements from the STAVKA reserve. '. . . ferocious, unparalleled tank battles ensued on the flats of the steppe, on hills, in gorges, gullies and ravines, and in settlements . . . The scope of the battle was beyond all imagination. Hundreds of panzers, field guns and planes were turned into heaps of scrap metal. The sun could barely be seen through the haze of smog from thousands of shells and bombs that were exploding simultaneously.' Lieutenant-General Dragunsky commented: 'Towards the evening of 8 July, one regiment had only ten tanks left. The adjacent brigade had to withdraw to another sector. Our tank regiment was no longer able to hold its position. Communications to the battalions was interrupted and we were running out of armour-piercing shells. Also, there were many wounded. One would think we were on an island in the midst of a sea of fire. It was senseless to stay in this sector any longer. We had to make our way to the main forces of the brigade.'

In the early morning of 9 July Hoth launched an attack with more than 500 tanks along a 10-mile front between Verkhopenye and Solotino. Deploying in wedges of between sixty and a hundred panzers, with the inevitable Tigers at the point, the Germans launched themselves once more against the armour of 1st Tank Army and the riflemen of 6th Guards. By late evening the Germans had at great cost succeeded in pushing the Soviet line back to within just twelve miles of Oboyan. German losses, however, had been very severe; the Soviets estimating that this effort had cost them some 230 tanks and assault guns destroyed and nearly 11,000 men killed. 'Grossdeutschland' had barely 100 tanks fully operational. In the late afternoon of 9 July Hoth began a regrouping of his forces as the emphasis of Fourth Panzer Army's assault shifted northeastward from Oboyan towards Prokhorovka. Moves were afoot that would lead within a few days to the clash of two mighty bodies of armour, in what was to become 'the greatest tank battle in history'.

Army Detachment 'Kempf'

Throughout 5 July III Panzer Corps and 'Raus' Special Attack Corps had struggled through the 3-mile-deep minefield and the strong defensive works between the River Donets and the railway, but the bulk of the armour did not cross the river until nightfall. This first day had seen extremely heavy fighting, Shumilov's 7th Guards Army yielding ground only grudgingly. Throughout the night the divisions of III Panzer Corps were

deployed with 6th Panzer to the rear of 7th Panzer Division. At dawn on 6 July 19th Panzer Division supported by the main body of 168th Infantry Division advanced against the firmly entrenched heights to the north-east of Belgorod. Severe fighting took place here for the next three days with the Germans maintaining heavy pressure on the Soviet forces, but it was only when 6th and 19th Panzer Divisions, acting in concert, broke through in the direction of Melikhovo that the Red Army units were finally dislodged from the Belgorod heights. The deployment of the German armour was characterized by great fluidity, divisional boundaries being shifted and subsumed where necessary to allow an effective response to the immensely powerful and very well-camouflaged Soviet units on the ridge; while deep in the minefield 6th and 19th Panzer Divisions actually managed to encircle and destroy two Soviet rifle divisions.

The previous day had seen General Breith, the commander of III Panzer Corps, come to a decision of some significance, when he abandoned the original plan to drive east and seize Korocha. The Soviet defences lying to the east of the Donets and blocking the axis of advance towards the town were too powerful. Breith decided not to expend time and effort to break them, given the very critical timetable that Hoth had imposed on the movements of the Corps armour. If III Panzer Corps was to be in place to assail the southern flank of the Soviet armoured reserve when it clashed with Fourth Panzer Army in the vicinity of Prokhorovka, it was necessary to devote all the efforts of the Corps to that end. Breith therefore ordered 7th Panzer Division to wheel north to support the drive of 6th Panzer Division, to whom he gave the central task of breaking through the Soviet defences and driving as hard as possible towards Prokhorovka. As the axis of advance of the entire Corps shifted northwards, the formerly defending Soviet units, began a series of strong attacks all along the extending eastern flank of III Panzer Corps. To the south of the main advance the flank was held in a series of blocking actions by 106th and 320th Infantry Divisions, which executed great damage against the troops of the Volchansk Group as they tried to break into the

▲10th Tank Corps's T-34s were used by General Katukov, commander of 1st Tank Army, to counter-attack the powerful German forces launched against Oboyan on 9 July. Heavy fighting took place with very heavy tank losses on both sides. The Soviets were determined to block the German drive to take Oboyan whatever the cost. (Novosti)

▼Panzer IIIs and IVs from 11th Panzer Division, Fourth Panzer Army advance against the forces of Chistyakov's 6th Guards Army covering the approaches to Oboyan. A tank battle of major proportions began as Soviet armoured reinforcements from the STAVKA reserve were released to block the German drive to take the town and its all-important bridge across the River Psel. (Bundesarchiv)

rear of the German front. As the battle proceeded, 7th Panzer found itself increasingly functioning as a mobile flank guard, screening the drive north-wards of 6th Panzer Division. Even though success was now attending the arms of III Panzer Corps as it moved north, it was still, on 9 July, embroiled in fighting in the Soviet defence lines. In the afternoon, while Hoth was regrouping the forces of Fourth Panzer Army in preparation for his thrust towards Prokhorovka, the advance units of Rotmistrov's 5th Guard's Tank Army was already moving into its assembly positions to the north-west of the town.

10 July: Ninth Army/Central Front

Although German forces had continued to assail Ponyri throughout 9 July, the failure of the assault on Teploye and the Olkhovatka heights on the 8th caused Model to spend the day regrouping his forces. He intended to attack again on the 10th and had already moved forward 10th Panzer Grenadier and 31st Infantry Divisions to support the continuing assault on Ponyri. These divisions were his last reserve units, and their committal

would mean that he had no forces available in the event of an emergency. While there may have been some in Ninth Army who still thought it possible to breach the Soviet lines with one last effort, the tone of the telephone conversation between Zhukov and Stalin early on 9 July was such that apparently the Soviets were already convinced that the Germans no longer had the resources to achieve their objective. It was decided that the Bryansk Front and the left wing of the Western Front would launch an attack on the German forces in the Orel Bulge on 12 July to force the Germans to draw off forces from Ninth Army. Central Front would then begin its own counter-offensive in the hope of catching the German forces off balance before they had time to organize their own defences. Although Rokossovsky realized that his troops would have to face a few more days of German fury, it was accepted that would be the last, desperate, flailing attempt of an Army that was in reality already defeated.

Under a leaden sky, in wind and driving rain, the final German attempt to break through to Kursk from the north began. Once again the objective was the Olkhovatka heights. Preceded by

Panther ausf D. 'Citadel' marked the début of the Panther, where its appearance was less than auspicious, more being put out of action by engine fires and mechanical problems than were destroyed by Soviet firepower. The early Model D at Kursk was identifiable by the flap in *the glacis for the machine-gun, and the drum type cupola. Later Model Ds carried the cast cupola as on Models A and G.*

◄ Not the least of the problems facing Model was that the Soviet Air Force had been very successful in attacking the supply lines of Ninth Army, notwithstanding strong Luftwaffe support. Even while his final attempt to break through the defences in front of Olkhovatka was under way on the 11th, the German divisions involved were having difficulty in obtaining supplies as a consequence of the Soviet air effort. (Novosti)

a tremendous artillery barrage and massed air support from Stukas and Heinkel He 111s, the 300 panzers of 2nd and 4th Panzer Divisions deployed to assault the last Soviet defences strung along the ridge. On the bare plateau before the Soviet positions were the same minefields and other defensive obstacles with which the German soldiers had become so painfully familiar during the previous five days. The infantry, on foot on this occasion, were rapidly left behind by the panzers and found themselves exposed on terrain devoid of any natural cover. Here they fell prey to the dug-in Soviet infantry, massed artillery fire and air attack. Losses began to mount rapidly. Many panzers were destroyed by T-34s, either dug-in or functioning as mobile fire points. Others repeatedly turned back to give their infantry cover and support, but were destroyed by anti-tank gunners sited invisibly in the cornfields. Although some local successes were attained, by evening the attack

had shot its bolt and Model ordered Ninth Army over to the defensive, except at Ponyri. In a little over six days Model had lost more than 400 tanks and 50,000 men to effect a penetration that nowhere exceeded more than fifteen kilometres.

Army Group South/Voronezh Front

Although throughout 10 July XLVIII Panzer Corps maintained heavy pressure against the remnant of Chistyakov's 6th Guards Army and a depleted 1st Tank Army covering the approach to Oboyan, in Hoth's wider scheme of things the purpose of this operation was to distract Soviet attention, and mask the disengagement of the SS Panzer Corps which, after a rapid regrouping, would shift the axis of its attack to the north-east and Prokhorovka. Notwithstanding the very heavy fighting between the divisions of XLVIII Panzer Corps and the Soviet forces to the west, Vatutin had already surmised Hoth's intentions. STAVKA had informed him that XXIV Panzer Corps, the Army Group reserve for the battle and comprising SS 'Wiking' and 10th Panzer Divisions, was already under orders to move north from Kharkov in preparation for operations. SS 'Totenkopf', now completely disengaged from its flank cover duties, had been moved across the rear of 'Leibstandarte' and 'Reich' and stationed on the left of the SS Panzer Corps. Late in the afternoon of 10 July, Third Battalion, First Panzer Grenadier Regiment of 'Totenkopf' cleared the last remaining Soviet bunkers in its assembly area, crossed the River Psel and established a small bridgehead on the northern bank. Despite intense Soviet fire and efforts to dislodge them, the men of 'Totenkopf' pushed forward and by late evening had secured the village of Krasny Oktabyr. The significance of this move lay in the fact that the Germans had managed to breach the last defensive barrier covering the advance to Kursk. With the crossing secured, and heavy bridging equipment being thrown across the Psel, the option of wheeling north into the rear of the Soviet positions on 11 July was now possible. By nightfall, although depleted and certainly weakened as a consequence of five days of very heavy fighting, the resupplied

and regrouped SS divisions were nevertheless able to deploy nearly 600 tanks and assault guns for the coming attack. The very narrow sector of the German attack, amounting to no more than six miles at its widest point, allowed Hausser to deploy nearly 160 panzers and assault guns per mile, an immense concentration of offensive power. It was this phalanx of armour and the sheer ferocity of the SS assault, allied to a genuine threat posed by 'Kempf's' forces approaching from the south, that was to delay Vatutin's own plans for a counter-offensive. Initially to have been launched on the 12th, this was to have involved Zhadov's 5th Guards Army and Rotmistrov's 5th Guards Tank Army attacking to the south-west from Prok-

▼*Seen here in conversation with senior officers of 2nd SS Panzer Grenadier Division 'Das Reich' is Obergruppenführer Paul Hausser, commander of II SS Panzer Corps. A former Army general, Hausser had been invited by Heinrich Himmler to organize the Verfügungstruppe(VT), the original 'Special Purpose Troops' from which the Waffen SS evolved. At the time of Kursk Hausser was still under a cloud with Hitler for disobeying his order to stand and fight at Kharkov in February. Indeed, Hausser was not to be exempt from the Führer's recriminations in the aftermath of the defeat at Kursk. (Munin Verlag)*

horovka in conjunction with the reinforced 1st Tank and 6th and 7th Guards Armies in a series of concentric blows designed to encircle the German forces in the salient.

During the early afternoon of 10 July Vatutin received the information that Hill 244.8, on the road to Oboyan, had been seized by 11th Panzer Division. The storming of this position was to mark the northernmost point of the German offensive in the south of the salient, and was the climax of a most eventful day for XLVIII Panzer Corps. Having repaired the damaged bridge at Verkophenye and constructed another bridge able to take tracked vehicles during the night of 9/10 July, 3rd Panzer Division was able to cross the Pena in the early morning and rapidly assail the units of the Soviet III Mechanized Corps on the Berezovka heights. With 332nd Infantry Division advancing from the south, resistance collapsed. By the end of the 11th the bend of the Pena had been cleared and the German line pushed further to the west. Nevertheless, as the main axis of the German push shifted from Oboyan to Prokhorovka and more Soviet units entered the line, XLVIII Panzer Corps found itself once more up against strong, reinforced defences and very frequent counter-attacks. Apart from small local advances, the line on this sector of Fourth Panzer Army's front was to remain as it stood on 11th July, until the German withdrawal began some days later.

▲Early on the morning of 11 July the SS Panzer Corps rolled forward towards Prokhorovka. On the left wing of their thrust the panzers of 'Totenkopf' found themselves heavily engaged with Soviet forces. Clearly visible on the right, next to the driver's armoured cover on this Panzer IV Ausf 'G', is the Totenkopf Kursk divisional marking – three vertical bars. To the left can be seen other Mark IIIs and IVs of the division. (Bundesarchiv)

Not the least significant of the events that occurred on the 10th, although some thousands of miles from the battlefield in the Ukraine, was the Allied landing in Sicily. With 160,000 British and American troops ashore in the first wave, that which the German generals had feared and against which von Manstein had constantly warned had now come to pass. While the OKW situation report phlegmatically recorded the event, it also announced the continuation of Operation 'Citadel'. It was obvious, however, that it would not be very long before the consequences of Operation 'Husky' would have an impact on the offensive in Russia.

11 July: Ninth Army/Central Front

Early on Sunday 11 July, Army Group South launched its great attack towards Prokhorovka. In this complex operation, the attack by Army Group

Panzer IV. It was in the spring of 1943 that the Panzer IV ausf H illustrated here was introduced. Upgunned with the 75mm L/48, the most distinctive feature of this model was the addition of schurzen (skirt armour). These were a direct response to the introduction of the Soviet

RPG-1943 shaped-charge anti-tank grenade and provided the panzer with a modicum of 'stand-off' protection. Camouflaged in the by now standard sand colour with red-brown and green, the Panzer IVH moving en

masse across the steppe is one of the dominant images of the Panzerwaffe in action at Kursk.

South against the Voronezh Front was to coincide with another attempt by Model's Ninth Army to break through the Soviet lines in the Olkhovatka sector, but here German hopes were to remain unfulfilled. Heavy probing attacks by Soviet Forces in Second Panzer Army's sector of the Orel bulge and to the rear of Ninth Army put a brake on Model's plans. Continuing throughout the day and growing in strength, these reconnaissance probings were clearly the harbinger of a major Soviet offensive, but von Kluge had no reserves with which to respond, all having been committed to action with Ninth Army. His forces were already stretched very thinly throughout the Orel bulge and he had little choice but to order panzer and motorized infantry divisions northwards from Ninth Army to deal with this contingency. By midday Rokossovsky began to receive reports that German units could be observed disengaging from Model's assault formations in front of Olkhovatka and moving north. This had been envisaged by

Zhukov, for by the time the Bryansk Front launched its offensive against Second Panzer Army in the early hours of 12 July, these German units would still be on the march to their new positions.

Army Detachment 'Kempf'/Voronezh Front

To the south of II SS Panzer Corps the three panzer divisions of Army Detachment 'Kempf', supported by assault gun brigades and the Tigers of schwere Panzer Abteilung 503, began their drive northward at first light on 11 July. Only the day before these units had still been enmeshed in the Soviet defence zone, but on the 10th 'Kempf' had succeeded in crashing through the last line between Melikhovo and the Sasnoye station. Breaking out into open country at last, the three panzer divisions then proceeded to assault the Soviet positions to the south of Prokhorovka with such success that the resistance facing III Panzer

◀ *Rotmistrov's 5th Guards Tank Army would be the main Soviet force to bear the brunt of the SS Panzer Corps' attack on 12 July. Following the outbreak of the war he had seen service as chief of staff, 3rd Mechanized Brigade. In January 1942 he became commander of 3rd Guards Armoured Brigade and in April he was again promoted to become commander of 7th Armoured Corps. In February 1943 he became commander of 5th Guards Tank Army.*

▲ *In the evening of 11 July Lieutenant-General Pavel Rotmistrov was forced to commit two tank brigades to prevent the town of Prokhorovka falling into German hands. Here T-34s attack the German lines with infantry support. The 'square' containers on the rear of the T-34s are spare fuel containers. By late evening the Soviets had seen off the German attacks but both sides now prepared themselves for the major clash that would come on the following day. (Novosti)*

Corps collapsed. As dusk fell on the 11th, some 300 panzers and assault guns were approaching Prokhorovka from the south.

II SS Panzer Corps/Voronezh Front

Shortly after III Panzer Corps began its drive northwards, the SS Panzer Corps began its own advance towards Prokhorovka. The 600 tanks and assault guns of the Waffen SS crashed into the Soviet screening forces in front of the town.

Overhead the Luftwaffe flew endless sorties throughout the day and late into the night. The ferocity and power of this attack wrong-footed the assembling Soviet forces detailed to begin their own counter-offensive on the 12th. Throughout the day the Waffen SS panzers brought very heavy pressure to bear in front of the town. Lieutenant-General Rotmistrov, whose 5th Guards Tank Army and attached 2nd Tank and 2nd Guards Tank Corps, was moving into its assembly area, relates how he and Marshal Vasilevsky had encountered the advancing Germans. 'Although it was toward evening, the bombings by German aircraft did not stop. Riding in a jeep, we crossed a grove and saw the buildings of a state farm on the right. Ahead of us, about one half mile away, dozens of tanks were moving along the road. Vasilevsky ordered the driver to pull up at the edge of the road and, looking at me sternly, asked me in an unexpectedly sharp voice, for he was usually even tempered, "General Rotmistrov, what's happening? Why are the tanks moving ahead of time?" I looked through my binoculars. "They are German tanks." "Then they may deprive of us of our foothold and, what's more, they may capture Prokhorovka."' An immediate counter-attack by two armoured brigades restored the situation. By the end of the day Rotmistrov's tanks and the riflemen of Zhadov's 5th Guards, who had come into the battle straight off the march, had by dint of very heavy defensive fighting held off the German armour. Despite this temporary reprieve the Soviets were clearly facing a situation of great potential danger. To wait until 1st Tank and 6th Guards Armies were fully reinforced and Zhadov's 5th Guards Army was properly deployed before opening the counter-offensive against Hausser's SS divisions would allow time for Kempf's 300 tanks and assault guns to reach Prokhorovka. With a mass of German armour totalling nearly 900 machines bearing down on the town from the west and the south, the entire Soviet position could unravel, with disastrous results. Vatutin therefore ordered Rotmistrov to prepare for an immediate counter-attack on the SS Panzer Corps for 12 July. In addition, 11th and 12th Mechanized Brigades of 5th Mechanized Guards Corps together with 26th Armoured Brigade of 2nd Guards Corps, and

92nd Guards Rifle Division, were ordered to counter-attack and block at all costs the further advance of III Panzer Corps, while the bulk of 5th Guards Tank Army launched its own heavy attack on Hausser's SS divisions the following morning. Throughout the short and dismal night the tank crews on both sides laboured to load and refuel their machines for the great trial of strength that lay ahead.

12 July: The Tank Battle of Prokhorovka

The sound of tank engines warming up could be heard long before dawn. A low, almost tangible throbbing could be sensed, signifying the presence of two immense bodies of armour, soon to clash in the greatest armoured confrontation in history. As the morning light broke across the landscape, visibility was obscured by local showers falling from a sky of leaden clouds, driven by a cold eastern wind. Periodically the sun would break through, allowing the observer a clearer perspective, to scan the lie of the land in what was clearly a very constricted arena of combat. For the commanders of the SS Panzer Corps, standing in the turrets of their tanks, a panoramic sweep of the battlefield would have shown its northern boundary firmly anchored by the winding ribbon of the River Psel. Swinging south-east the view would have taken in a traditional, slightly rolling steppe landscape characteristic of the Upper Donets valley, with fields of rye and wheat broken here and there by the small, cultivated plots of collective farmers, by hedges and the odd wooded copse. Farther to the east and barely three miles away lay the agricultural town of Prokhorovka, its tall grain silo standing proud against the skyline. The southernmost boundary of the battlefield, only four miles from the Psel, was fixed by the cutting of the Kursk–Belgorod railway, for to its immediate south the land became hilly and broken up by mounds and ravines, rendering it unsuitable for large-scale tank warfare.

Rotmistrov had set up his command post on a small hill south-west of Prokhorovka from where he could observe the unfolding battle. It opened with the appearance of large numbers of Luftwaffe aircraft bombing the Soviet positions. In the wake

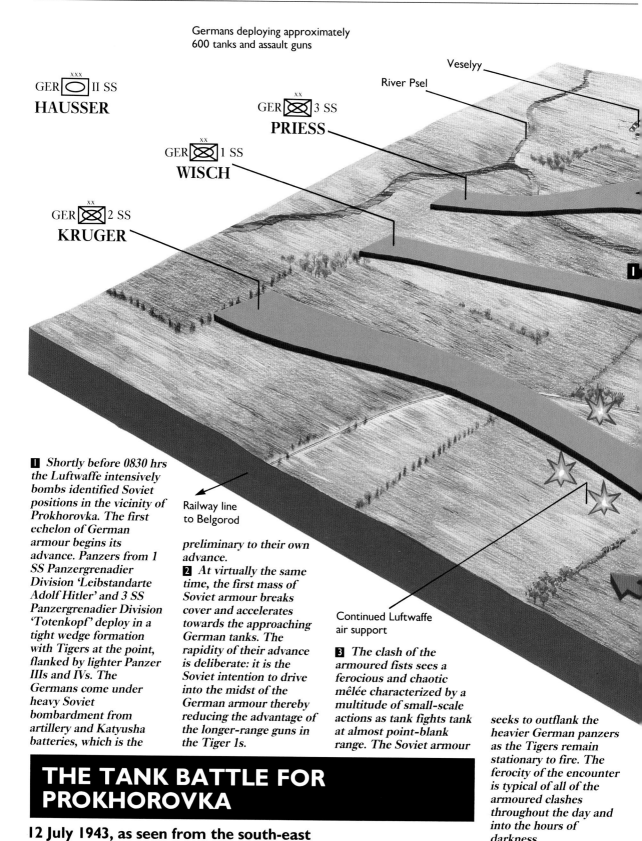

Germans deploying approximately
600 tanks and assault guns

Veselyy

River Psel

GER [xxx ⬭] II SS
HAUSSER

GER [xx ⊠] 3 SS
PRIESS

GER [xx ⊠] 1 SS
WISCH

GER [xx ⊠] 2 SS
KRUGER

1

Railway line
to Belgorod

Continued Luftwaffe
air support

1 *Shortly before 0830 hrs the Luftwaffe intensively bombs identified Soviet positions in the vicinity of Prokhorovka. The first echelon of German armour begins its advance. Panzers from 1 SS Panzergrenadier Division 'Leibstandarte Adolf Hitler' and 3 SS Panzergrenadier Division 'Totenkopf' deploy in a tight wedge formation with Tigers at the point, flanked by lighter Panzer IIIs and IVs. The Germans come under heavy Soviet bombardment from artillery and Katyusha batteries, which is the preliminary to their own advance.*

2 *At virtually the same time, the first mass of Soviet armour breaks cover and accelerates towards the approaching German tanks. The rapidity of their advance is deliberate: it is the Soviet intention to drive into the midst of the German armour thereby reducing the advantage of the longer-range guns in the Tiger 1s.*

3 *The clash of the armoured fists sees a ferocious and chaotic mêlée characterized by a multitude of small-scale actions as tank fights tank at almost point-blank range. The Soviet armour seeks to outflank the heavier German panzers as the Tigers remain stationary to fire. The ferocity of the encounter is typical of all of the armoured clashes throughout the day and into the hours of darkness.*

THE TANK BATTLE FOR PROKHOROVKA

12 July 1943, as seen from the south-east

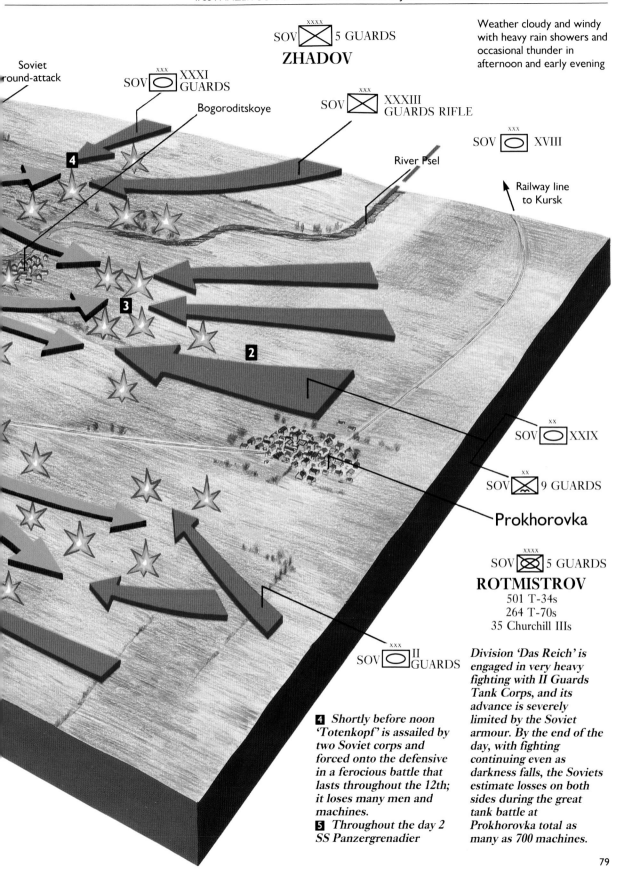

SOV ⊠ 5 GUARDS
ZHADOV

Weather cloudy and windy with heavy rain showers and occasional thunder in afternoon and early evening

Soviet round-attack

SOV ⬭ XXXI GUARDS

Bogoroditskoye

SOV ⊠ XXXIII GUARDS RIFLE

SOV ⬭ XVIII

River Psel

Railway line to Kursk

4

3

2

SOV ⬭ XXIX

SOV ⊠ 9 GUARDS

Prokhorovka

SOV ⊠ 5 GUARDS
ROTMISTROV
501 T-34s
264 T-70s
35 Churchill IIIs

SOV ⬭ II GUARDS

4 *Shortly before noon 'Totenkopf' is assailed by two Soviet corps and forced onto the defensive in a ferocious battle that lasts throughout the 12th; it loses many men and machines.*
5 *Throughout the day 2 SS Panzergrenadier*

Division 'Das Reich' is engaged in very heavy fighting with II Guards Tank Corps, and its advance is severely limited by the Soviet armour. By the end of the day, with fighting continuing even as darkness falls, the Soviets estimate losses on both sides during the great tank battle at Prokhorovka total as many as 700 machines.

79

of the aircraft the first mass of German armour, some 200 tanks, could be seen moving in from the north-west. SS 'Totenkopf', its Tigers to the fore and flanked by the lighter Mark IVs and IIIs, advanced in a tight wedge formation, followed by the tanks of 'Leibstandarte' and 'Das Reich'. At approximately 0830 the Soviet lines erupted as a 15-minute artillery and Katyusha barrage crashed down on the German defences. As the front line disappeared in a hurricane of fire and smoke, the 500 tanks of Rotmistrov's 5th Guards Tank Army's forward echelon broke cover and accelerated towards the advancing avalanche of panzers and assault guns. Acutely conscious of the quali-

tative advantage of the Tigers and Panthers over their own T-34s, Rotmistrov had ordered his tank commanders to close the distance by driving hell for leather at the advancing German armour so as to negate the German advantages in gun range and armour. While deploying a numerical superiority of just under 900 tanks to Hausser's 600, the German force could adequately compensate by the technical superiority of its Tigers and Panthers. Indeed, not all of Rotmistrov's tanks were T-34s. Of the total number of tanks deployed by 5th Guards at Prokhorovka, only 501 were T-34s; 264 were light T-70s and 35 British-supplied Churchill IIIs. Each corps of the Tank Army had a

▲In the early morning under an overcast sky, the SS Panzer Corps armour begins its advance on Prokhorovka. Heavy

artillery has already begun to range in on the advancing Panzer IIIs and IVs of 'Das Reich'. (Bundsarchiv)

▼The heavy smoke drifting across the battlefield lends an eerie quality to these Tiger 1s attempting to range in at

the very fast moving Soviet tanks, now racing to hit the forward screen of the SS Panzer Corps' armour. (Bundesarchiv)

▶ *5th Guards Tank Army's T-34s had to close with the leading panzers very quickly to get them within range of their own 7.62cm guns. Exploiting the smoke and the terrain as these T-34s are doing here, the Soviets were able to get among the Tigers and Panthers and fire into their thinner side armour. At these very close ranges the result was often catastrophic, tanks of both sides erupting in huge fireballs as their fuel and ammunition exploded. (RAC Tank Museum)*

regiment of SU-76s, but Rotmistrov had none of the formidable new SU-152s.

'The sun came to our aid. It picked out the contours of the enemy tanks and blinded the German tankmen. Our first echelon at full speed cut into the positions of the German troops. The appearance on the battlefield of a great number of our tanks threw the Germans into confusion. Control was soon disrupted. Our tanks were destroying the Tigers at close range, where the Germans could not use their armament to advantage in close combat. We knew their vulnerable spots, so our tank crews were firing at their sides.

The shells fired from very short distances tore large holes in the armour of the Tigers. Ammunition exploded inside them, and turrets weighing many tons were flung yards away.' By 0900 the bulk of the armour of both sides was already engaged and the fighting degenerated into one huge, wild, swirling mêlée, with packets of armour on both sides using whatever cover could be found to extract some little advantage, in the murderous slogging-match. Soon the battlefield was littered with the shattered remains of gutted armour. Thick, black oily smoke from destroyed tanks drifted across the battlefield and made gunnery

The Soviet Offensive Against the Orel Bulge, 12 July to 18 August 1943

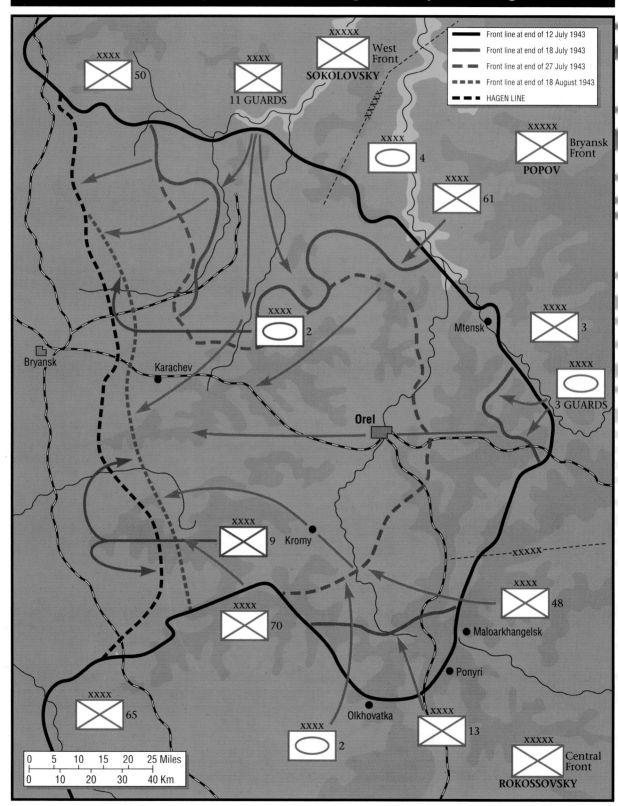

Front line at end of 12 July 1943
Front line at end of 18 July 1943
Front line at end of 27 July 1943
Front line at end of 18 August 1943
HAGEN LINE

XXXXX West Front SOKOLOVSKY

XXXX 50

XXXX 11 GUARDS

XXXX 4

XXXXX Bryansk Front POPOV

XXXX 61

XXXX 2

Bryansk

Karachev

Mtensk

XXXX 3

XXXX 3 GUARDS

Orel

XXXX 9 Kromy

XXXX 48

XXXX 70

Maloarkhangelsk

Ponyri

XXXX 65

Olkhovatka

XXXX 2

XXXX 13

XXXXX Central Front ROKOSSOVSKY

0   5   10   15   20   25 Miles
0   10   20   30   40 Km

◀ *The Soviet Offensive Against the Orel Bulge, 12 July to 18 August 1943. Since April 1943 It had been the Soviet intention to await the German offensive against the Kursk salient, ride it out, destroying the German armour in the process, and go over to the counter-offensive once it was known that all German reserves had been committed. By 9 July Stalin and Zhukov were already convinced that Model's offensive might had been irreparably damaged. On 12 July Operation 'Kutuzov' was launched against the German forces in the Orel Bulge by the left wing of the West and Bryansk Fronts. It had been hoped to co-ordinate the counter-offensive in the north with that in the south, but this was not possible because of the much higher losses sustained by Voronezh Front. It was this major threat to the German position in the Orel salient that led to the suspension of 'Citadel' on the 13th. Hitler gave Model command of Second Panzer Army as well as Ninth Army. The very strong defences the Germans had created in the 'Bulge' slowed down the Soviet drive and their attempts to encircle the German forces within came to nought. Although suffering heavy losses the Germans were able to conduct an orderly fighting retreat to the 'Hagen Line' which was complete by 17/18 August. Nevertheless, since 5 July Army Group Centre had lost the equivalent of fourteen divisions, and these were irreplaceable.*

T-34 Model 1943. The most numerous Soviet tank employed at Kursk was the T-34. However, all mounted the 76.2mm gun, which placed them at a disadvantage against the guns of the Tiger and Panther, the upgunned 85mm version not seeing action until the autumn of 1943. This T-34 Model 1943 was used by Lieutenant-General A. G. Kravchenko, GSS 5-i gvardyeiskii tankov'i korpus during the battle. It carries spare 76.2mm ammunition in boxes on the hull sides and spare fuel box containers at the rear. This vehicle uses the arrangement of rubber rimmed and solid steel wheels seen on many intermediate production T-34 Model 1943s.

▲*Taken after the battle of Prokhorovka, this photograph shows very well what happened to the heavy panzers if T-34s managed to 'kill' them at very close range. This Panther 'D' of 'Das Reich' has had its turret lifted from the hull by a massive internal explosion. (Novosti)*

▲ Although the image of Prokhorovka is one of a titanic clash between hordes of German and Soviet armour, there was also a vicious and bitter battle going on between the infantry of both sides with infantry teams stalking tanks. Here a Soviet anti-tank rifle team fire at panzers from the lee of a destroyed SS Panzer Corps Panther. At the close ranges which characterized the fighting at Prokhorovka, even anti-tank rifle ammunition could be lethal. (Novosti)

▼Another post-battle image. These Soviet tankers are no doubt discussing the Tiger they 'killed'. The number of hits on the turret armour and the manner of its cracking illustrate the degree to which these tanks could absorb punishment. The shell that did the job looks to have been a 7.62cm fired from a T-34 at close range. (Novosti)

difficult for both sides. There were more than a few instances of Soviet tank crews deliberately ramming German armour, the resulting detonation and concussion being felt across the battlefield as ammunition and fuel exploded in a huge fireball. Overhead the fighters of both sides wove their deadly dance, trying to destroy one another, and large numbers of ground-attack aircraft dipped low over the battlefield to strafe enemy armour and supporting infantry.

On the left flank of the SS Panzer Corps, 'Totenkopf' was involved in some of the most vicious fighting of the day. Having advanced early, the bulk of its armour was engaged in a ferocious fire fight, when shortly after mid-morning it encountered a large formation of Soviet reserve armour. Wheeling, advancing, stopping to fire and firing on the move, the tanks slashed at one another at point-blank range. Armour, rent asunder by internal explosions and venting sheets of flame, rained shards of metal all over the battlefield. Shortly before midday the Soviets committed a further two corps from the reserve and 'Totenkopf' was assailed by 31st Guards Tank and 33rd Guards Rifle Corps, and forced on to the defensive. But the division held and prevented the Soviet armour breaking through the blocking position established by the troops, though at a cost

that by the evening of 14 July amounted to more than 50 per cent of the division's men and equipment.

Throughout the early afternoon the SS Panzer Corps maintained the pressure, but at great cost. 'Das Reich' found its ability to advance hampered by repeated attacks from the tanks of 2nd Guards Tank Corps through the gap that existed between its right flank and the advancing III Panzer Corps. Time and again the Panthers, Tigers and other armour were pinned down when formations of T-34s and T-70s launched themselves at the SS division. As the colossal contest continued, it was becoming clear to Hoth, now present on the battlefield with 'Der Führer' Regiment of 'Reich', and Rotmistrov, observing events from his command post, that the matter could be swung by the arrival of the panzers of Breith's Corps. Although a surprise *coup de main* on the night of 11/12 July had enabled the Germans to seize a bridge over the Donets at Rzhavets, they were unable during the course of the afternoon of the 12th to penetrate the defences established by the Soviet units dispatched to block their advance. By the time III Panzer Corps had got through the Soviet screen on the following day the crisis had passed. A last surge, by the 'regrouped' 'Leibstandarte' and 'Reich', directed at breaking 18th Tank Corps to

▶ *The only heavy tanks that 5th Guards Army had available for the battle at Prokhorovka were thirty-five Lend Lease Churchill Mark IIIs. These were given short shrift by the SS Panzer Corps. In common with much of the armour supplied by the Allies, they were profoundly disliked by Soviet tank crews for being much too slow and for having a weak main armament. (Bundsarchiv)*

the west of Prokhorovka, was met by the commitment of the final reserves from the second echelon of 5th Guards Tank Army. In a repeat of the clashes of the morning, 10th Mechanized and 24th Guards collided head-on with the panzers. Smoke and dust darkened the sky. Separate shots could not be heard as all the sounds blended in a continuous, terrific roar.

Although fierce fighting continued for the rest of the day and only died down at nightfall, the Soviets had succeeded in stopping the German attack. As Rotmistrov observed: 'More than 700 tanks were put out of action on both sides in the battle. Dead bodies, destroyed tanks, crushed guns

▶ *Operation 'Rumantsyev': The Soviet counter-offensive against Belgorod and Kharkov. German withdrawal in the face of heavy Soviet pressure led to Vatutin's forces re-occupying by 23 July all territory lost to the Germans during 'Citadel', but Soviet lossess had been far higher than in the northern sector of the salient so the planned co-ordination of the northern and southern counter-offensives could not take place. Vatutin was unable*

to launch 'Rumantsyev' until three weeks after 'Kutuzov' had begun. The operation began on 3 August. During the next three weeks very intense battles were fought around Kharkov which the Germans finally abandoned on 22 August. On 15 September a very reluctant Hitler gave von Manstein permission to withdraw Army Group South behind the Dnieper. The German Army had begun a retreat that would not end until the fall of Berlin twenty months later.

◀ *After the battle German equipment littered the battlefield. Much was shattered or damaged beyond repair, but those tanks that could be repaired were used by the Red Army against their former owners. (Novosti)*

Operation 'Rumantsyev': The Soviet Counter-Offensive Against Belgorod and Kharkov

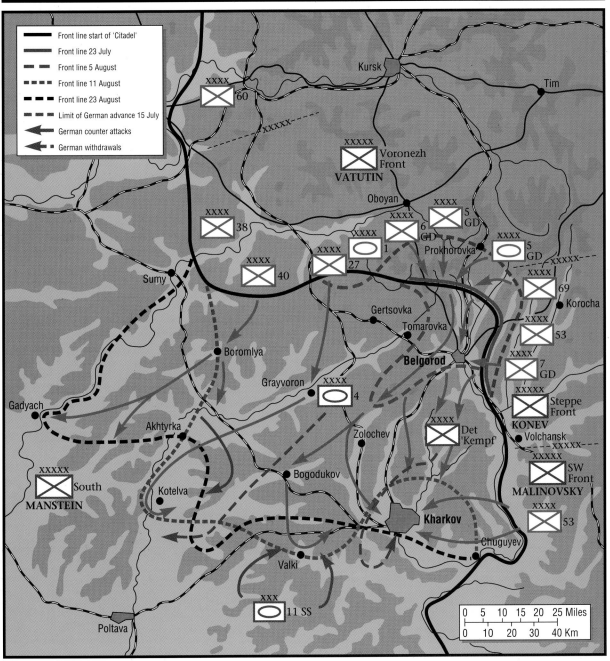

and numerous shell craters dotted the battlefield. There was not a single blade of grass to be seen; only burnt, black and smouldering earth throughout the entire depth of our attack – up to eight miles.' In this most aptly named *Prokhorvskoe poboishche* (Slaughter at Prokhorovka), more than 50 per cent of 5th Guards Tank Army was destroyed, but for the Germans the losses were proportionately far greater. A total of 300 panzers including many Tigers lay abandoned on the battlefield, together with 88 guns and 300 trucks. Most had been destroyed, but even those that normally would have been recovered and put back into service were lost to the Germans, because the battlefield remained in Soviet hands. Although the next few days(13 to 15 July) would see repeated efforts by the SS Panzer Corps to generate some success out of the ruins of the 12th, they were at best residual attempts to inflict further heavy losses on the Soviet armour, and draw at least some of the teeth of the coming Soviet counter-offensive in this sector. In reality, by the 13th Hoth, Hausser and von Manstein knew that 'Citadel' had been abandoned.

13 July: The Wolfsschanze

The day after Prokhorovka, von Manstein and von Kluge received orders to report to Hitler at his headquarters in East Prussia. It was clear from the Führer's demeanour that the situation in Italy had him very rattled. The requirement for divisions to protect Germany's southern flank led to his announcement that he intended to suspend 'Citadel'; the divisions he needed could only be found among those engaged in in Russia. Furthermore there was growing evidence of a Soviet build-up opposite Sixth Army and First Panzer Army defending the Donets basin. Von Manstein argued that victory in the south was within reach, and

proposed that he and von Kluge relaunch the offensive, leaving some divisions of Ninth Army in place to tie down Soviet units. But it was von Kluge, now having to contend with a large-scale Soviet offensive launched in the early hours of 12 July which had already made deep inroads into Second Panzer Army's front, who finally sealed the fate of 'Citadel'. He needed Model's forces to contest the growing Soviet offensive threat, and he stated that he would not be able to resume the offensive against the Central Front. The most that von Manstein could extract from Hitler was the compromise that Hoth be allowed to continue his attacks, so as at least to inflict a partial defeat on the Soviets. But in the decision to suspend the offensive, Hitler was admitting that 'Citadel' was beyond recovery and that the Germans had, indeed, sustained a decisive defeat.

▼*Hitler called off 'Citadel' on 13 July. The Soviet counter-offensive had been launched in the Orel Bulge on 12 July. In the south, Vatutin launched his somewhat later, but by 23 July, only ten days after the end of 'Citadel', the Soviets had recovered all the ground lost to the Germans. This scene of German prisoners of war was to become more and more common as it became very clear that at Kursk the Germans had lost the strategic initiative.*

▲In a rash of offensives, embracing all the Soviet fronts that covered Army Group South, the Red Army pushed westwards so that by December the front line stood far to the west. In this photograph the SU-152, the notorious 'animal hunter', carries infantry in an advance that would not stop until the Red Army reached Berlin.

▼As Guderian had predicted, Kursk was a decisive defeat for the Germans. Exact tank losses are difficult to pin down. In July returns indicated that 645 tanks and 207 assault guns had been destroyed. In August a further 572 tanks and 143 assault guns were lost. By October, when the Soviet offensive broke down, the Germans had lost more than 2,500 armoured vehicles. Only one-third of all the armoured fighting vehicles available to the Army at the beginning of 'Citadel' remained in service.

THE AFTERMATH

The great prize for the Soviet Union in defeating the Germans at Kursk was the gaining of the strategic initiative. After Kursk there were no further German offensives in the East. From the launching of the counter-offensives that eliminated the limited gains the Germans had made in the salient by the end of July, the Soviets sustained an advance against the Wehrmacht that did not end until the Red Flag was hoisted over the Reichstag, in Berlin, in May 1945.

There can be no doubting the fact that the German Army inflicted very heavy losses on the Red Army during 'Citadel'; Soviet tank strength after the battle was down by 50 per cent. Set against the balance sheet of strategic gains and losses, they were the price that Stalin and Zhukov were prepared and expected to pay for the destruction of the German armoured forces. Soviet estimates of German losses are far higher than those given by German sources. While this is not surprising, given that each side had its own axe to grind, the Germans did acknowledge the fact that their losses at Kursk had a decisive impact on the outcome of the war in the East. As the war in the East was the decisive theatre of operations in the European War as a whole, it follows that at Kursk the Germans sustained the defeat that lost them the war.

Since the battle there has been a tendency for Kursk to be explained away as a German defeat rather than a Soviet victory. While this view can be accounted for partly by the manner in which 'cold war' perceptions have influenced historical judgements, it is nevertheless a demeaning and false analysis. In all the factors that determined the outcome of the battle the Soviets held the whip hand. It was they who dictated the battlefield and the nature and form of the battle. While it is true that mistakes were made during the course of the battle – they admit as much themselves in postwar accounts – the Red Army was nevertheless moving very quickly up the learning curve. In the end, the most pertinent observation concerning the outcome of 'die Blutmühle von Belgorod' was that made by Hoth to von Manstein: 'The Russians have learnt a lot since 1941. They are no longer peasants with simple minds. They have learnt the art of war from us.'

CHRONOLOGY

Events leading to the Battle of Kursk

22 June 1941 Hitler launches Operation 'Barbarossa', the invasion of the Soviet Union.

5 December The Red Army launches its great counter-offensive in front of Moscow.

June 1942 'Case Blue', the German summer offensive, begins in southern Russia.

19 August German Sixth Army ordered to capture Stalingrad.

23 November Soviets surround Sixth Army in Stalingrad.

31 January 1943: Sixth Army surrenders at Stalingrad.

8 February Soviets retake Kursk.

16 February Red army retakes Kharkov.

17/18 February Hitler visits von Manstein's headquarters at Zaporozhye; tentative discussions concerning coming summer campaign; gives go-ahead for Manstein's counter-offensive.

22 February Von Manstein launches German counter-offensive between Rivers Dnieper and Donets.

15 March II SS Panzer Corps retakes Kharkov.

18 March Germans recapture Belgorod. Von Manstein's proposal to continue advance on Kursk from the south and effect an encirclement of Soviet forces in the region in conjunction with Army Group Centre quashed by the refusal of von Kluge to co-operate in the operation. Further German offensive action called off in face of Soviet resistance and the onset of thaw.

8 April Zhukov submits key planning document to Stalin in which he sets out reasons for containing German summer offensive in a *defensive* battle; key aim is destruction of the German panzer force.

12 April Stalin reluctantly accedes to desire by Zhukov and other senior commanders to fight Germans in defensive battle; orders go out to fortify Kursk salient to receive German offensive.

15 April Top secret Operation Order No. 6 detailing outline for Operation 'Citadel' authorized by Hitler; states earliest date for the offensive as 3 May 1943.

April–July Hitler repeatedly delays launch date for 'Citadel'.

12 May Axis forces in Tunisia surrender.

Battle of Kursk

5 July Operation 'Citadel' begins. In the north and south of the salient German forces make very small gains in the face of massive Soviet resistance and strong defences. No operational objectives laid down before battle opens are realized.

7–10 July *Ninth Army*: Model's main effort directed at seizure of the settlement and heights of Olkhavotka. Immensely powerful German forces batter at Soviet defence lines inflicting, but also taking, very high casualties and losses. Assault on village of Ponyri likened to a miniature 'Stalingrad'. Model unable to make decisive breakthrough to Kursk. Early on 9th, Stalin orders Zhukov to launch offensive against Orel Bulge on the 12th. *4th Panzer Army*: On the left, XLVIII Panzer Corps manages to seize crossing over Pena by 9th. On the 10th, 'Grossdeutschland' seizes Hill 244.8, most northerly point taken on advance towards Kursk. SS Panzer Corps having fought its way through Soviet defence lines regroups on 10 July in order to direct attack against Prokhorovka. Soviet reserve forces from Steppe Front moving in strength towards same place. *Army Detachment Kempf*: By 9th these forces have at last managed to penetrate Soviet forces screening advance northwards. Heavy fighting as detachment moves north towards Prokhorovka.

10 July Allies land in Sicily.

11–12 July *Ninth Army*: Model commits his last reserve to attack on Ponyri on 10/11th. Indications of major Soviet offensive against Orel bulge forces

Kluge to draw off German units from Ninth Army. Offensive by Ninth Army to all intents over. *4th Panzer Army:* On 11th, SS Panzer Corps begins drive on Prokhorovka. The 12th sees one of the largest tank battles ever fought as SS Panzer corps clashes with 5 Guards and 5 Guards Tank Army at Prokhorovka. Some 700 German and Soviet tanks destroyed. *Army Detachment Kempf:* Soviet pressure prevents Kempf joining Hoth on battlefield at Prokhorovka.

13 July Hitler calls off 'Citadel'. Massive Soviet offensive against Orel Bulge.

Aftermath
17 July Hitler orders SS Panzer Corps out of the front. Soviets begin offensives on Army Group South right flank.
23 August Soviets retake Kharkov.
7 September Germans begin evacuation of the Ukraine.

A GUIDE TO FURTHER READING

Kursk is not one of the best documented battles of the Second World War notwithstanding its significance in relation to its outcome.

Carell, Paul. *Scorched Earth*. George Harrap & Co Ltd., 1970

Clark, Alan. *Barbarossa*. Hutchinson & Co, 1965

Erickson, John. *The Road to Berlin*. Weidenfeld & Nicholson, 1983

Jukes, Geoffrey. *Kursk: The Clash of Armour*. Purnell's History of the Second World War: Battle Book No 7, 1968

Koltunov, Colonel G. A. *Kursk: The Clash of Armour*. Purnell's History of the Second World War, 1966

Manstein, Erich von. *Lost Victories*. Methuen & Co Ltd., 1958; Arms & Armour Press, 1982

Piekalkiewicz, Janusz. *Operation 'Citadel'*. Costello, 1987

Ziemke, Earl F. *Stalingrad to Berlin – The German Defeat in the East*. Dorset, 1968

WARGAMING KURSK

Kursk is certainly a battle that catches the wargamer's imagination. The sheer size of the forces involved, the unprecedented concentrations of armoured and air forces, the resources invested in minefields and fortifications and, not least, the appreciation on both sides that the clash would be of decisive importance for the future course of the war – all contribute to the sense of doom-laden drama evoked by the name, Kursk.

Yet, although much spoken of, Kursk is rarely wargamed. In common with many other decisive battles (Leipzig, Gettysburg, El Alamein) Kursk was a 'slogging match' between evenly balanced opponents; there was little scope for sweeping manoeuvre in this grinding battle of attrition. Wargamers seem to be attracted by the idea of a game about Kursk but to lose heart once they look at the battle a little more closely. In fact, however, there is plenty to stimulate and challenge the wargamer. In this section, let us examine where the drama really lies and how it can be reflected in games.

Essentially the excitement of Kursk lies in the time-pressure facing the Germans. For the last time they are able to assemble the great bulk of their striking power in Russia, trained, equipped and prepared to a standard they will never see again. They possess immense strength, far more than they will have in 1944, but every battle will wear them down. Their opponents have gained vastly in numbers since New Year 1943, but many units lack the skill and experience possessed by their Wehrmacht counterparts. The question is whether the superbly skilled German military machine can break into open country to fight a mobile war before the burgeoning but largely inexperienced Russian reserves can strangle it within the confines of the fortified zones around the Kursk salient. In wargames the German should always be driving his force to make a final effort while the Russian agonizes about whether or how to commit his local reserve.

Boardgames

Perhaps for some of the reasons outlined earlier, Kursk is treated thinly by boardgame manufacturers. Back in 1971, Avalon Hill's *Panzerblitz*, a tactical Eastern Front game using tank platoons on 250 metre hexes, contained a scenario based on the tank battle at Prokhorovka. This was supplemented by the 'roll your own' market with a larger game comprising scenario-specific terrain maps and counters for the full order of battle. Although highly popular when it first appeared, *Panzerblitz* lacks any form of command and control mechanism and possesses some very odd visibility rules (which are, however, easily amended). The attritional nature of Prokhorovka is reflected, as is the limited scope for surprise and manoeuvre.

At about the same time the American boardgame company SPI produced *Kursk*, a game about the entire battle in the salient using divisional-level counters and turns lasting several days. The game is now out of print but is the only boardgame, I know of that covers the whole battle. It is more successful at portraying the set-piece German assaults than the mobile battles that followed but does illustrate the scale of the operations and the growing power of the Red Army.

Apart from these games, Kursk normally features as a scenario in most of the strategic level Eastern Front boardgames, such as Avalon Hill's *Russian Campaign*. There is much to recommend this approach as the Kursk battle can be seen in its proper context. One can argue that the Battle of Kursk began during the spring of 1943 as Army Groups North and Centre conducted tactical withdrawals and thinned out their lines to provide troops for 'Citadel'. For their part, the Russians saw the blunting of the German attacks in July merely as a prelude to their own summer offensives. Timing was an important governing factor the success of offensives on both sides, each seeking to calculate how far the other had committed its reserves before launching their own blow. A strategic game enables these elements to be introduced.

One problem that greatly reduces the value of boardgames as a simulation, however, is their open nature. In any game it is clearly difficult to achieve surprise or create uncertainty if all the units are deployed in full view of both players. This can be overcome by the use of one or more umpires and maps.

Wargames

In a typical tabletop or boardgame the two players administer the rules themselves while playing the game. If more people are available, however, a game can be designed in which the players can concentrate on the command decisions while an umpire deals with the rules. In this way the 'fog of war' can be recreated rather more convincingly than is normally the case with a two-player game. There can be moments when the action slows, as the umpires huddle, but there can also be moments of very great tension, not to say panic! The basis of the umpire-moderated game, and indeed of most wargames between 1824 and 1960, is the *Map Kriegsspiel*. In this type of game the players, or player teams, occupy separate rooms while one or more umpires act as go-betweens. As the name implies, the action is carried out on maps marked with chinagraph pencils, but if they have time the umpires may find it more convenient to use a modern terrain with markers. It can be easier to move solid models around than to keep scrubbing out chinagraph pencil markings or to compute lines of sight, and to weigh up terrain factors on a three-dimensional display rather than on a map. It is therefore quite possible that with this technique the players will be using maps, as the real commanders did, while the umpires will be manipulating something that looks very like a tabletop wargame.

Scenarios for this type of game are numerous, but Army Group Centre's offensive in the Orel salient would be fascinating. Can General Model break through north of Kursk before 61st and 11th Guards Armies attack it from the north? Should they attack early to relieve the pressure on their comrades in the Kursk salient or should they wait and attack when Model is fully committed? Fourth Panzer Army's offensive would be a classic mapgame. Moves would be daily, and the action would be resolved at divisional or brigade level. The later, and smaller, mobile battles around Kharkov also offer a great deal of interest.

The Phone-In Wargame

Organizing the personnel for a multi-player game can be difficult. People have to get together on the same evening, possibly from widely spread locations. There can be other logistic difficulties in providing accommodation, food and so on. These inconveniences can be eased because it is not actually necessary for all the people to get together in the same place; all that is necessary is that they are able to communicate with each other. During a map game the umpires communicate constantly with the players, sometimes by written message, but for the most part their communications will be verbal and delivered during a visit to the player concerned. If each participant has an identical map with a grid system, then reference to any point on it can be made without the necessity for a visit. If players and umpires are connected by telephone they can pass all the messages they want while distanced from each other by the width of a corridor, a county – or even a continent.

The phone-in wargame is very simple but highly effective. About two weeks before the game, contact the participants and arrange a date for the event. Devise a scenario and issue maps and briefings. Allow the players enough time to send in a written plan to you so that you can set up your map, and just before the game issue updated intelligence assessments to each player. Then the game can proceed with phone calls in a sequence:
1. Get Orders from attackers,
2. Get Orders from defenders, adjudicate combats, etc.,

3. Give feedback to attackers and get fresh orders,
4. Give feedback to defenders and get fresh orders.

Put a limit on the duration of each call. This encourages players to keep orders short and saves you money!

The phone-in game does require that each player make fairly extensive use of his telephone for the evening. Do not play on the evening that the mother-in-law calls unless you want to simulate a sudden communications blackout! Apart from the domestic strife that could arise, readers may feel that the bills incurred for a succession of 20-minute conversations would make the game prohibitively expensive. This is not actually the case, as reference to telephone charge rates will demonstrate – unless players are actually located in Moscow or Berlin. The cost could, in any case, be split among all the participants.

Tabletop Games

The tabletop is not, at first glance, the ideal way of wargaming battles on the great open spaces of the Eastern Front. For one thing, commanders at the higher levels considered in this book generally fought their battle from maps rather than by seeing the action on the ground; for another, a tabletop tends to give the players too much information. Nevertheless, it would be true to say that German divisional commanders and below, as well as Russian commanders, did spend quite a lot of time visiting units on the ground in pursuit of that elusive *Fingerspitzengefühl* (or 'fingertip feeling'.) for the battle. Furthermore, despite the great areas over which the battles were fought, the attack frontages were quite small; between 2 and 5 kilometres for large armoured formations.

At 1 inch:100 metres it should be quite possible to recreate the area of a German divisional or Russian corps-sized attack for games using 1:300 scale figures. There will be a lot of vehicles involved (perhaps 3,000 per side), so the model scale will have to be adjusted or a differently sized tactical unit used on either side. We might use one model for each platoon, company or battery, which will make the game much more manageable, although we need to remember that at most levels models will be needed for the supply columns, engineers and other units that do not often appear in other wargames. A little care is required in devising the scenario. If there is to be a major German attack the chances are that it will make some progress; the game will then be about the Russian counter-attack, so the table needs to be deep enough to accommodate it. The Russian forces should be kept off the table until they are spotted by the Germans. An historical example of this type of battle is to be found in General von Mellenthin's book *Panzer Battles*. In the opening stages of the attack XLVIII Panzer Corps, with 'Grossdeutschland', 3rd and 11th Panzer Divisions, attacks a single Russian rifle division, but the Russians throw in mechanized and tank corps on successive days to stop them. Who will give way first? It is important not to allow the game to bog down, even though the real battles did! The game should be a tense one for the commanders as they try to achieve objectives against time pressures. Keep the pace of the game high by having relatively few moves and bringing in different events to keep up the tension – rainstorms, air attacks, fresh troops, etc., so that the commanders always have a fresh problem to deal with.

A different scenario might try to depict a Russian rifle division in defence along the table. None of the Russian forces are placed on the table except outposts. The Germans, with a larger force, must locate as many strongpoints, minefields, etc., as possible by patrolling, local attacks, aerial reconnaissance, prisoner interrogation, raids and so on, to a time limit. Once this is up they must plan their big offensive. The defender must try to outguess the attacker and deploy his scanty reserves in the right place – once the offensive gets going it may be difficult for him to move units around under heavy air and artillery bombardment. An umpire is needed for this fascinating intelligence game, but it is possible to have a two-player game by not playing the defending side. An umpire could draw up a defensive layout and reactions, which he would then disclose according to the attacker's moves against it. In some games the umpire could run the Russian side entirely because the Russian army was relatively stereotyped in the conduct of its attacks. Some readers may be familiar with the 'one player-one umpire' technique from the boardgame *NATO Division Commander*.

A third scenario might concentrate on the mobile battles characteristic of the July–August period. The Russian player might start at the end of the table with a sketch map and a large force, such as a tank corps, with orders to get to the other end within a certain time limit. The table should give him a choice of routes to his objective. The German player receives a more detailed and accurate map and a smaller force, with some panzergrenadiers, anti-tank guns and a few tanks. He will first have to find which route(s) the attacker is using before deploying his forces. These can remain hidden until located by the enemy and must make use of concealment and ground to delay the Russians for as long as possible.

Megagames

In recent years a number of wargame clubs have combined their resources to run very large map games using fifty or more participants. Recent megagames set on the Eastern Front have been set at German corps / Russian army level with four-man teams playing commander, operations, intelligence and logistics staff officers. A higher level command team at German army / Russian front level has done its best to control proceedings via a system of intercoms. These games require a lot of time and energy to prepare if they are to be run successfully, but they can offer players an unusual opportunity to exercise a degree of real 'command' since they will need to work as a headquarters team. The presence of an actual 'human factor' means that morale becomes not merely a modifier to be applied to a die roll but can be seen on the faces of the 'enemy' on the other side of the hall! Success can only be achieved if teams organize themselves to absorb the flow of information and then issue coherent orders that coordinate the activities of all their units – and those of their colleagues.